21 Things You Forgot About Being a Kid

21 Things You Forgot About Being a Kid

a partial guide to better understanding our children and ourselves

Dr. Rick Stevenson

5DP

5000 Days Publishers
Burien, Washington 98166

© 2019 by 5000 Days Publishers

Published by 5000 Days Publishers, an imprint of
HJ Books
P.O. Box 48282, Burien, WA 98166
www.hjbooks.com

Printed in the United States of America

ISBN: 978-0-9787554-8-5

Contents

Foreword

I MAY BE SLOW, but it finally hit me. The realization began a couple years ago when I marked my 5000th interview with kids and teens in my 5000 Days Project, and resurfaced again recently when I was interviewing a 13-year-old, fatherless, aboriginal boy in Australia named XYZ. (Yes, that's his real name.) He assured me that he was going to be the one to rewrite his family's difficult history for the better. It came yet again as I witnessed one of my Cambodian girls struggle courageously to be who she is in a country that is not quite ready to accept her. And it came through Luciano, my Chilean kid, who after losing his right leg, right arm, and right eye now refers to his left side as his "lucky side."

What hit me was that **we own nothing more valuable than our own story.** Think about it. What else is there? And what is more important than discovering who we are and who we are meant to be?

Given the sheer number of these interviews that I have conducted, I was asked recently to give a series of TED-like talks about what I have learned. I have concluded that when we dare to tell the most difficult story we'll ever tell—our own—the benefits are endless.

First, it forces us to look at our own lives and determine if we are going to be the main character in our own story or a secondary character in someone else's. It's a choice. Every moment of every day through every action and every word, we author the real-time narrative of our lives—whether we recognize and own it or not.

Second, learning to tell our own story necessitates perspective—a bird's-eye view of the mountain road we travel called life. From the road itself, we see the beauty of the mountain, the danger of the cliff and the curve up ahead—and that's it. What we think lies around that curve is consciously or unconsciously determined by what we have encountered around previous curves. Learning to tell our own story requires the bird's-eye view—making sense of our past influences, as well as helping us define where we want and need to go.

Finally, learning to tell our own story is the key to a better world. In my interviews, when I get to the question of "What are your three wishes?," the grand majority of kids ask for "world peace"—that is, up until 12 years old. After that, the wish starts to sound naive to them. Having studied world peace for my doctorate, I know how elusive a political, economic, or social solution can be. But it was the ancient Chinese philosopher Lao Tzu who refused to let any of us off the hook. To paraphrase, he said "there will never be peace between nations until there is peace within nations; there will never be peace within nations until there is peace between neighbors; there will never be peace between neighbors until there is peace within families; and there will never be peace within families until there is peace within our own hearts." In other words, if we each take care of making the content of our own stories the best it can be, we can change our world from the bottom up. In this way each of our stories is epic and essential.

As I completed writing these talks, my wife Julie put it all in perspective for me. She pointed out how much I've grown personally from these interviews. The thought suddenly occurred to me: "Oh, my gosh! Do I have thousands of kids around the world helping me work out my issues?" Well, yes. I do. And you know, I'm okay with that!

I have marveled watching each member of my immediate family—Julie, Max, Whitney, Madee, Leah and Oliver—make the everyday choices that write their stories. The struggle, the pain, the joy, the triumph— what an extraordinary canvas the Universe has given us upon which to paint. And it is the way in which these stories become interwoven like some vast tapestry that makes them particularly beautiful.

My hope is that this book not only celebrates the young people whose stories have inspired it but also encourages readers to write their own epic stories through their own words, thoughts, and actions each and every day.

Rick Stevenson
Vancouver, B.C., Canada
July 1, 2019

Introduction

I BLAME IT ALL on Jackie Kennedy. When I was 7 years old and she was America's first lady, I was crazy in love with her. I became convinced that she was the ideal woman, and that someday I would marry her. Now, I was only marginally naive. I knew that she was already married to that JF-whatever guy, but for some reason that did not seem to be an impediment at age 7.

But first impressions of love and perfection die hard. My parents had a wonderful marriage and, from as early as I can remember, all I wanted was to meet the woman of my dreams and have a family. Evidence the fact that when I was 8 years old, I suddenly started suffering from stomach ulcers. The doctors blamed it on too much worrying. My mother told me of nights during that year when I could not sleep due to concerns about being unable to afford to buy my future wife a wedding ring! Yes, strange but true.

Cut to thirty years later. I'm in my late 30s and have had countless dates and numerous relationships but am still no closer to finding the woman of my dreams than I was at age 7. I was not a "player"—I was just lacking self-knowledge about my actual problem. I can only imagine now what a hopeless date I must have been.

In fact, it was at the three-year mark of one of my relationships when my then-girlfriend, frustrated by my inability to commit further, asked if I'd go into therapy with her. My reply was telling, and classic. "Therapy is for people with *problems*," I said. She gave me that look— yes, *that* one—and I said, "Okay."

Three weeks later, we were broken up and I got to keep the therapist.

That was the beginning of my realization that I had not been the master of my own emotional life— instead, ignorance had been my master. While my Oxford credentials suggested at least a respectable IQ, my EQ (emotional-intelligence quotient) was pathetically low.

To illustrate: My therapist, Donna Arnold, an empathetic but no-nonsense woman a few years my senior, took me through family-of-origin work. This involved a mental data dump to paper—writing down every memory I could dredge up from the recesses of my mind.

The real whopper of ignorance came when Donna had me recall all of the women I had dated in detail. After an exhaustive description of each relationship, she said, "Rick, you talk of all these women in such glowing terms. They sound terrific. So what was the problem?" I shook my head frustrated. "I don't know, I just never felt the absolute certainty that any of them was the right one." Donna nodded then asked me a simple, observational question: "So, Rick, what do all of these people you dated have in common?" I thought a moment then replied, "They were all women?" She looked at me patiently and recommended I think deeper. After a long moment I replied, "Me? I'm what they have in common?" She nodded and said, "Yes. Did you ever consider that *you* might be the problem?"

The question hit me like an atomic blast of white light. And as with a blast of white light, I was, in that moment, able to see the world around me, including myself, with absolutely clarity and focus. I had been raised with such a positive self-concept that this dawning did not offend me on any level. In fact, the revelation that it was *me*—something that was so simple and so painfully obvious to everyone around me—set me free and launched me on a lifetime quest to solve the rest of the mystery that was me.

That was the beginning of a beautiful relationship with discovering my own story. Through the process, I learned all sorts of things.

First and foremost, I learned that my perfect WASPish family was not so perfect after all. There was no ill intent, however. In fact, quite the opposite. My parents were the most sincere, kind, well-meaning people alive. They had grown up during the Great Depression and had an epic love story involving three chance meetings against the backdrop of the Second World War. My father was a well-loved superintendent of schools, eventually becoming a major figure in education on a national scale. My mother was a reading specialist and my greatest advocate. Unlike a lot of kids, my sister Jody and I never had reason to question how well or how much we were loved. We were blessed.

Despite all of that, we seldom spoke the truth in our family. We didn't exactly lie; it's just that verbal conflict was such an anathema in our white-bread family that we constantly spoke in subtext, avoiding important issues that might offend. In fact, I never remember hearing my parents fight. Hence, when my first girlfriend and I got in a fight, I broke off the relationship believing that it must be doomed. Only later would I learn that "fighting" was part of the currency of a healthy relationship—one based on honest emotions and a mutual trust in the process.

Ultimately, what I discovered was that in my most intimate relationships—the ones I had with my family—I was constantly surrendering the truth and myself to the cause of harmony. Hence, intimacy represented a loss of self, and at a certain point I would go running from every relationship as a means of self-preservation.

Understanding that fear was the first step in conquering it. Through this work I did with Donna (which continues off and on to this day), I was able to make fundamental changes in myself and prepare myself to at long last be a worthy mate. To cut to the chase, along came Julie—a funny, bright, honest, and beautiful woman, four years my junior with two beautiful kids (Max and Madee). She was that attractive woman in the grocery store that men would look at—but she would be totally unaware because her focus was her kids. For that reason she had little interest in dating, but out of respect for a mutual friend who had wanted to set us up she luckily relented and went on a date with me. I had a feeling on the first date, as did she, that this one was different. When I asked her to marry me just past the turning of the millennium (12:03 am January 1, 2000), I had never felt more certain about anything before in my life. First date to marriage was six months. I had wasted enough time due to my own ignorance. Now I was going to make up for it.

And now that I had what I had always wanted and more, I decided I needed to find a project that might keep me in Seattle, Washington. I had spent the previous 25 years producing, writing, and eventually directing television and movies everywhere but at home in Seattle.

I decided a documentary might be the answer despite the fact that I had never made one before. The decision was largely financial. Around that time, advances in technology made it possible for me to own my own gear and back my own project without needing a studio or a financier. I just needed a topic. Having long been a fan of the BBC *Seven Up!* series in which Michael Apted had interviewed a series of British kids across the spectrum of class every seven years from age 7, I concluded that local kids would be fun to film—especially now that I had two of my own. Despite my affection for the *Seven Up!* series, though, I had always been a bit frustrated that Apted only filmed the principals once every seven years; hence, we never fully understood the changes they experienced. I was also frustrated that the interview questions were not terribly deep, and worried by the fact that the very act of broadcasting a documentary seemed to have a deleterious effect on a few of the subjects' lives.

To this end, I first came up with the idea of filming kids once a year so as to create a kind of time-lapse portrait of growing up—what researchers call a "longitudinal study." In fact, the "5000 Days" Project was born based on the loose number of days it takes for a child to go through school.

Second, I consulted with teachers, psychologists, and specialists, most notably my friend Dr. John Medina, who wrote the *Brain Rules* series of books. I wanted to compile the list of ultimate key life-questions—questions that kids are never asked on a regular basis. And I wanted those questions to be nourishing and nurturing to the young interviewees. Not the type that just "use" them for documentary purposes.

Finally, knowing how personal and important each story was to each child and wanting to make sure the project produced healthy kids, not victims, I decided to leave the rights in their hands. I would own the footage itself, but they would own the rights—and hence we would have to come to a secondary mutual agreement before any story was made public.

This, of course, had not been done in documentary filmmaking before—primarily due to the fact that films cost a lot of money to produce, and spending tens of thousands of dollars filming people over a decade only to have them decide not to tell their stories was not exactly a winning business plan. I realized it would make the overall project almost impossible to finance. However, if I was going to ask kids to share deeper than kids had ever shared before on film, I needed to guarantee them that right. It was simply the proper thing to do. So with Julie's full support, I committed to earning outside money nine months a year and paying the Project's costs ourselves.

I approached the Shoreline School District in North Seattle with the idea, and their enthusiasm was extraordinary. They asked if they could recommend a few kids via key teachers… and they ended up recommending *roughly 800*. I interviewed all of them and selected 60 based on their willingness to be honest, open, and articulate.

The first interviews were in February 2001 and the second set was in December 2001. Of course, what happened in between was 9/11, and that event changed everything. I learned that kids not only wanted but *needed* to talk on a much deeper level. Since most of us remember exactly where we were and who we were with in the immediate aftermath of 9/11, we also remember the palpable fear that it bred. The roar of an engine in the sky, a column of smoke rising in the distance, a series of violent images that can never be erased; they all left an indelible imprint on us.

With the kids' permission, we showed some of the results of the first year's interviews at the district's Schools Foundation fundraising breakfast. Something amazing occurred. Educators approached me *en masse* asking if the process could be made more widely available—because it was clear that kids who went through it were processing their fears and expectations better than those who had not. The idea was further bolstered by encouraging notes from two young public servants who were present: Patty Murray, who would become Washington State's first female senator, and Jay Inslee, who would become governor. Subsequent meetings confirmed the impact and, as a result, the 5000 Days Project went through a radical pivot from being just a documentary to becoming an initiative aimed at helping kids process what they are feeling, and why they are feeling it. All of this would be aimed at helping them become the masters of their feelings versus the victims.

Word got out—eventually resulting in the Project being invited into schools across the city, then the state, then the country, and then the world. We have now touched all six inhabitable continents, over a quarter of a million interview clips are currently being stored by our

StoryQ scaling technology, and my annual in-person "Ambassador" interviews involve kids from twelve countries. Of course, this involves a great deal of travel and has completely gone against my original plan to pursue a project that would keep me at home. Fortunately, however, my family has gone with me on many of these adventures and my younger kids had traveled to six continents by the age of 11.

Cut to today. At time of this writing, I have now conducted over 5500 in-depth personal interviews with kids and teens over almost two decades. As I was considering the strengths and weaknesses of my anecdotal approach to discussing this work, a professor friend recently remarked, "I may base my books on studies, but none of us in academia have had boots on the ground, getting dirty, conducting 5500 first-hand interviews with kids. Who is to say whose conclusions are more accurate, let alone scientific?" With full respect and appreciation for my academic colleagues who toil admirably through various studies and, with full acknowledgement of the limitations of my own approach, I present the following.

I have had the advantage of learning some astounding lessons from my 5000 Days kids about what they want and need. And that is the purpose of this book. To pass those on. So here we go… Twenty-one things you forgot about being a kid…

One is the Loneliest Number

You feel completely alone, certain that you're the only one going through what you're going through—the only one feeling what you're feeling.

SHE SAT IN FRONT of me, barely holding it together. At 12 years old, Ella was still the picture of innocence, but the secret she was about to share weighed heavily on her small, sloping shoulders. "I've been looking at porn," she whispered as the tears began to fall. "It just came up on my computer. I didn't look for it—but I looked at it. And I liked it." And then she broke into heavy sobs.

After she was able to regain her composure, I asked her how liking porn made her feel. She said, "Kind of creepy, kind of good. Ashamed. Alone. Really alone. I'm close to my parents, but I could never tell them. I don't even know why I'm telling you."

"Maybe you're telling me because you don't want to feel alone," I suggested. "In fact, I think you *want* to tell your parents." She looked at me cautiously. "And, I think your parents would understand—because I can guarantee you that lots of kids, older and younger than you, have had this very experience."

She looked at me, shocked. "Really?" she said.

"Yes. What matters is what you decide to do from here."

■

DREW WAS A HANDSOME, gentle giant. Straight-A student, football captain, wise beyond his years, admired all around. When his good friend from childhood posted a suicide video and then killed himself with a shotgun as his parents entered the room, he was devastated. Despite the availability of grief counselors, Drew did not know how to process such a senseless act. Nor did his friends. He told me that, despite the availability of grief counselors, after four months his close-knit group of friends were still not talking about it with each other. As a result, everyone felt even more alone.

■

IT WAS 2009 AND the Great Recession was in full swing. The girl came into her annual interview looking distraught. After some discussion I discovered that her family was on the verge of losing their home. Her dad had been laid off and their savings had dried up. The tension had never been higher in the household. Mom and Dad were constantly fighting. She was paranoid about having to move schools and losing her friends. She was equally concerned about *not* moving schools and friends finding out about their situation. She could not talk to her parents or her friends. She carried these feelings of shame, alone.

What she did not know was that the previous four interviews the very same day had featured kids struggling with family image in the face of financial difficulties—all of whom shared a strange shame and panic, no doubt mirroring the feelings of the adults in their household. None of them had told anyone else about the situation. The economic crisis had struck hard and deep and *everyone* was suffering, as evidenced by the FOR SALE sign outside of our *own* house. Without naming names, I shared with her that everyone was feeling this way. She was stunned. "Really? For sure?" It gave her a small measure of comfort that she was not alone.

■

DURING HER ANNUAL INTERVIEW, 12-year-old Danielle talked about puddle-jumping, and the sheer joy of jumping in puddles and getting all wet. As for her aspirations, she looked forward to working with the mentally handicapped and changing their worlds. However, by age 13, she was in the depths of her own depression and grew worse over the next two years, eventually ending up in a mental hospital.

We sat down for an interview after a lapse of a year and a half, following her release. It turns out she was anything *but* crazy. As she revealed in the interview, she was simply burying a horrible event that happened one night in 7th grade when she and a friend were flirting with some older boys at a party. She ended up alone with a 17-year-old who locked the door and forced oral sex upon her. For the next two years, things unraveled as her secret was trapped in her own vault of shame and guilt. It was eating her like a cancer. Things got so bad that she eventually agreed to catch a bus to Moses Lake in Eastern Washington and sleep with a man she had met online—in exchange for 400 sleeping pills. She said goodbye to friends... and was tackled by a school security guard as she attempted to leave campus for the bus station.

By the time we got around to this interview, after a long dark road, Danielle was done with keeping secrets. They had almost killed her.

■

FOR A WEEK EVERY summer, I run the Prodigy Camp which, for the past decade, has been bringing together the twenty-five most talented teens in film and music from across the planet and giving them high-level training, a sense of social responsibility for their talent, and an opportunity to get in touch with their moral compasses. The center of the camp is Campfire 101 where the teens come tasked with the requirement to talk about the most difficult thing they've ever faced. Through the process, they find their voice and learn to tell the most difficult story they'll ever tell—their own.

It was the first campfire of the first camp when the youngest camper approached me, concerned. We had just heard an excruciating story about date rape and another about an older teen's initiation into a gang. The young camper was concerned that at his age, he had not experienced anything that had been a problem. I replied, "Well, I'm grateful for that, **Leo**. By the way, this is not a competition. It's just about the most difficult thing you've personally faced."

He thought a long moment, then shook his head, still coming up blank.

"For instance, I know that you live with your mom. How often do you see your dad?" I asked. He shifted a bit uncomfortably and replied, "Well, I don't really have a dad."

I looked at him curiously. "So you don't get to see him very much?" He replied again, "I don't really have a dad." I replied, "Are you saying you've never met him?"

Leo looked at me a bit uncomfortably, "I don't

really have a dad."

I said, "What do you mean you don't really have a dad? *Everybody* has a dad."

"My mom got a sperm donor." He looked at me, tentatively.

"Oh," I said, now understanding. I could see his face darkening. "Well, how do you feel about that?"

He hung his head and immediately burst into tears. I put my hand on his shoulder and told him that regardless how he made it on Earth, we were all grateful he was here. After a minute he said, "I've never talked to anyone about this before. Not even my mom."

I replied, "If you're up to it, I think you might have found your story."

The next night Leo shared his "origin" story and how grateful he was for his mom. He also shared that, despite it all, he was sad growing up without a dad. The other campers were immediately supportive,

commenting on how much his mom must have wanted and loved him to go to such lengths to conceive—but also how it sucked to grow up without a dad.

Leo went home and talked to his mother about it. It immediately brought them closer together. **Leo has**

gone on to be the most decorated, award-winning, young documentary film-maker in the USA. Now in his early 20s, he constantly chooses difficult topics that need to be discussed.

■

AS KIDS, WE ARE constantly being introduced to new, scary feelings for the first time—and never are those feelings scarier than when we are between 13 and 15. At that age, we feel too old to share certain feelings with our parents, and too young to share them with each other. This leads to the perfect storm of isolation— feeling lost and stranded on an uncharted desert island in the sea of anonymity. I don't know how many times I've seen pure astonishment and/or disbelief from young teens when I tell them absolutely everyone else is feeling exactly the same way they are feeling.

Most of us remember when at 15 or 16 we finally had that mind-blowing late night talk with either our best bud or a new friend, the one in which we find out we are not alone; and most of us remember the morning after, seeing the world anew, our life not looking as desperate as it had been hours before. I remember thinking to myself, "Why didn't I find this out *earlier*?"

Of course, the problem does not always end with our teens. I spent a year in London when I was 21 going to the London School of Economics. One cold winter day I was riding along a street of London row houses on the upper level of a double-decker bus. Night was falling and the bus was held up in the London rush-hour traffic. Exhausted, I momentarily closed my eyes then glanced to my right only to capture an intimate moment I'll never forget. Through the second-story window of a townhouse, I saw a 40-something woman sitting on her bed, leaning back against the shared brick wall that divided the houses. She was crying. I was moved by the apparent depth of her sadness and just how lonely she looked in her empty flat.

Then I saw a man around the same age, literally eighteen inches away on the other side of the same brick wall in a separate flat. He was leaning against the same wall, staring blankly into the growing darkness, one small light casting shadows about his room. He, too, was the picture of loneliness.

I don't know if it was my imagination or the empathy I felt for both of them but I wanted to scream, to get their attention, to let them know that there was another person in need less than a yard away. Who knows if they could have helped each other or even if it could have turned into the ultimate love story?

I do know that I was projecting some of my own loneliness, being on my own 4800 miles from home. The bus pulled away and I watched this intimate scene, this painful moment, retreat into the darkness of an autumn night.

I feel loneliest when I am troubled. I think we all naturally retreat and seek the safety of our walls. We want to hide our weakness and escape the risk of further exposure to the "outside world." In doing so, however, we cut off human connection—the very cure to our loneliness.

The Takeaway

What You've Forgotten About Being a Kid:
At times, you feel completely alone, certain that you're the only one going through what you're going through—the only one feeling what you're feeling.

What You Can Do About That as an Adult:
Be forthcoming with your own experiences of loneliness and share your own story. Doing so gives everyone else permission to share theirs— and shared stories are the anecdote to loneliness. If you're a parent, put good people around your children, and encourage them to find somebody they can trust and open up to… with full knowledge that it might not be you!

The Milk of Amnesia

You believe that your parents and other adults have absolutely no idea what it's like to be a kid today.

FACE IT: YOU ONCE thought that about your *own* parents. And now your kids believe it about *you*, too!

And guess what? *You were right.* And *your kids are right*, as well.

Evidence? At one point during your teen years you were likely told by some well-meaning adult, "Enjoy high school. It's the best time of your life." Even though you've probably forgotten and are now similarly waxing nostalgic about your own high school years, your initial reaction was probably like your kid's reaction today. Pure panic.

"*What?* Really? You've got to be kidding me. This is as good as it gets? Why am I even *here?*"

Middle school and high school have often been accurately compared to the Animal Kingdom—but our adult memories often cleverly transmogrify the experience into the Mufasa era of *The Lion King*. That's when all of the animals stand side by side singing and swaying to the music—when the Lion will lay down with the Lamb...

But we all know what the lion is really thinking! The expression on his face is not dissimilar of that to my teenage son when he stealthily retreats from the pantry to his room with the family's one bag of chips.

Despite being drunk on the milk of our own amnesia, we all rationally know that the rules of the animal kingdom are actually "eat or be eaten," a bit harsher reality than mere Natural Selection. Having done interview after interview and heard story after story, I am able now to clearly remember the abject fear I had going to Butler Junior High School every day in North Seattle. Yes, it was a suburban, largely white middle-class enclave... so it was quite naturally a haven for sex, drugs, and rock 'n' roll, and I wasn't ready for *any* of it. I was insecure about practically everything even though I came from a loving family, was tall enough not to get picked on, and had lots of friends.

But that was *then*, and not *now*. Did I have to live in a glass jungle where every move could be scrutinized and broadcast school and world-wide on social media? Did I have to drink from a fire-hose of information and misinformation coming at me with the force of a double-barreled hurricane? Did I have to resist the society-sanctioned addictions of video games, buzzing blue screens, and Internet porn? Did I have to worry about a gunman coming into my school and killing my friends *and* me at random? Thank God I did not. Things were wild enough in my day, so I can assure you that we as adults really have no idea what kids go through today. Not because it's more difficult now, per se, but primarily because it's just monumentally *different*.

So why do we as parents and adults keep coming out with such inanities as "High school is the best time of your life"? Pure hazing aside, my guess is that we do this for two reasons.

First, our brains tend to take the sharp edges off of humiliating or embarrassing events because the associated emotions are just too difficult to hold. Who wants to remember themselves as weak, indecisive, cowardly, or victimized? From the moment we are born we seek safety from things that threaten us. If we try to protect ourselves in the real world, why would we choose to dwell in dangerous memories? So we tell our kids things that we *wish were true*, rather than things that are actually true. And we're not even conscious of this whitewashing!

The second reason is that most of us carry deep emotional scars from our rough years that lead to various forms of arrested development. Without treatment to process traumatic childhood events, they either define us, or we suppress them altogether—both resulting in mental health problems.

For example: I was riding in the big black Hummer

of a contractor friend one day, looking at houses on a narrow, one lane street. We were unlikely friends on opposite ends of the political spectrum. But he loved his kids, I loved mine, and they were all friends—so we were friends, too. I knew he had a tender, emotional side to him, and I had seen him be incredibly generous to people.

However, on this day, like several others, I saw him retreat to the behavior of a wounded 10-year-old. He was driving so slowly that a line of cars had formed behind him. One dared to honk, and when I pointed this out, he said, "F*** 'em," and put his truck in Park, refusing to budge. I watched in shock as he got out of his truck, forcing the cars behind him to back down the street and find another route.

I saw this behavior *whenever* someone dared to challenge him. Later, we were talking about our childhoods and I learned that, as a middle brother, he had suffered constant abuse at the hands of his other two brothers. When? Around ten years old. He had gone on to develop a drug habit and live a rough life until he met someone with whom he had a beautiful family. Through sheer will power he was able to suppress past demons and become a caring father. But he was in a tough business, and when things got contentious his damaged 10-year-old self came out along with his fists. When things got contentious in his marriage, he didn't have adult skills to deal with adult problems, and things imploded.

Have you ever wondered why we're all so fascinated by coming-of-age films? Why the primary audience for Rob Reiner and Stephen King's *Stand By Me*—about four 12-year-old boys—was not kids but *adult men*? It's because most of us are stuck in some stage of arrested development from our adolescent years that we intuitively want to figure out. We're constantly walking around with loads of juvenile baggage.

A minor example of this is how most white people above 40 still define "health" as "a good suntan obtained while on vacation" despite the volumes of scientific evidence that prolonged exposure to the sun can kill us. We are so shaped by the values, challenges, and experiences of our youth that we tend to carry them for the rest of our lives.

Evidence of this arrested development is pervasive. The toxic masculinity that led to the #MeToo movement is largely a result of 30- to 60-year-old men acting like 14-year-olds with wads of cash and loads of power. Hollywood has often been referred to as "High School with money," and that's *not* a compliment.

Likewise, I have witnessed strong girls who wanted to be President of the United States when they were age 11 turn into insecure shadows of their former selves at 14, surrendering their self-worth to their attractiveness to men. And too many women get stuck there, never growing beyond their adolescent selves. As their physical beauty fades, they are left with little to rely on.

When asked what I've learned from 5500 interviews I've conducted with kids and teens, it probably would not surprise anyone to learn that, first and foremost... *I have learned a lot about myself.*

■

WHEN I FIRST STARTED the 5000 Days Project, I would often come home and just cry from the painful things I had heard. It seemed so unfair or so unacceptable that these kids had to experience what they were going through. However, as I soon discovered, the empathy I was feeling was grounded in my own suppressed feelings of anger, grief, frustration, sadness, anxiety, insecurity, and so on, from that very period of my own life. Interview after interview was opening up one arrested emotion after another.

This has led me to conclude that the generational divide we often feel with people of different ages is often much narrower than we may think. Yes, we have different levels of life experience—but we are all connected by a shared human emotional experience that is far stronger than the years that separate us. Just ask an 80-year-old couple how they first met, and watch them become like teenagers once again.

The beautiful thing about emotions is that, despite how scary and discomforting they can be, they are actually vital clues to the greatest mystery we will ever face: Who in the world am I?

A powerful example of this process at work involves my producer in the Cambodian 5000 Days Project, Mary-Anne Hatch. She was born to a Korean mother and an American father who had died in Vietnam. During our first year of the Project at the Sunrise Villages in Cambodia, we were interviewing a boy who had been trafficked to Thailand as a beggar at age 5. **When he dropped to his knees** to demonstrate how he used to beg, I heard Mary-Anne gasp and suddenly break down in tears behind me. When I asked her about this later, I learned that, when she was 7, her mother had told her to pack her bag for a holiday… and had then left her behind at a Catholic orphanage. She remembered dropping to her knees and begging her mother not to leave her in exactly that same way that our former beggar had demonstrated. The memory had been triggered when Mary-Anne saw herself reflected in this boy's story. Her catharsis solved a lifetime of mystery, helping her to heal and become who she was meant to be.

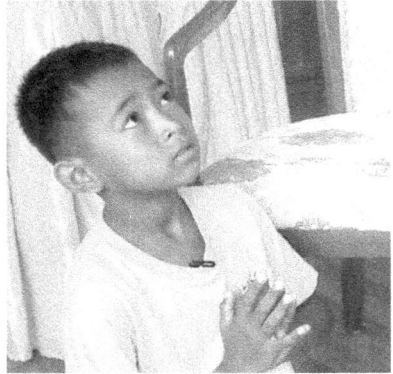

This reminds me that we *all* have questions to

answer; and when we dare to do so, our reward is unleashing the power of the most valuable thing we own. *Our own story.*

Are we destined to be clueless about what our kids are really going through? To some extent, the answer is yes. We will lack context when identifying with our kids' current journeys.

However, we can understand and connect with them better if we are willing listen and learn—if we stay in touch with them through emotions, that common language we all share. Not only will we find a deep well of connection in those shared feelings, but we open up the opportunity to further grow up ourselves!

The Takeaway

What You've Forgotten About Being a Kid:
As you're growing up, you believe that your parents and other adults have absolutely no idea what it's like to be a kid today.

What You Can Do About That as an Adult:
While some kids do have very good experiences in their teens, many do not. So don't expect them to. And don't get freaked out about their complex world. Learn about it, as much as you can. Listen. Talk to other kids their ages, many of whom want an adult to talk to (see Lesson

3). And then, be empathetic about the things going on in your kids' lives as you learn about them, without seeing yourself as "the fixer." Just be with them through it.

Lesson 3

If You Speak and No One Listens, Are You Making a Sound?

21 Things You Forgot About Being a Kid

You really want to talk to adults, especially your parents, but they don't show signs of wanting to listen.

WAIT! YOU SAY, *THAT sure is not my experience with my 14-year-old. Are you sure kids want to talk?*

Yes. A lot. And most of the time. Sadly, we all buy into a myth that kids, especially teens, don't want to talk—and I fear that becomes a self-fulfilling prophesy. As with many things, that's mostly on us as adults. I know that the sullen faces, tsunamic mood swings, one-word answers, and defensive body language suggest otherwise.

Witness my son, **Oliver**. At 7 years old, he was the picture of a boy who loves life, has a lot to say and wants to say it.

But at age 13, what do you imagine "that look" and

"that body language" tell you?

Yes, you're right. It says, "Go away. Don't talk to me. I want to be left alone."

But, like us, kids *lie*. And they speak in subtext.

I cannot tell you how many interviews I've had where kids say "…but I don't care," when they really mean, "I care about this more than anything else." Or when another is insisting, "I'm not sad; I'm really happy," while tears are running down their cheeks.

Kids saying they don't want to talk is the rare case where "No actually means Yes"—where "Leave me alone" really means "Don't leave me alone… I need you."

That does not mean they necessarily want to talk in the moment.

Remember that as teens we experience all sorts of new emotions (thank you, hormones!), and that we don't necessarily have the vocabulary to express them. Without that vocabulary, we fear we'll sound like an idiot. *However, emotions that go unexpressed gain power over us.* If our goal is to make our kids the master of their emotions, not the slaves, we need to provide a welcoming, non-judgmental atmosphere to talk. They need to learn that vocabulary from us.

But do we even have the vocabulary ourselves? I think the biggest barrier to our teens talking is that we as adults project the discomfort with not only teen subject matter (hello, arrested development!) but with articulating our own emotions.

I was raised with the vocabulary to properly express happiness, satisfaction, and harmony; but in my WASP home I was not raised with the ability to express anger or sadness. Neither were my parents. Nor *their* parents. Add this hereditary lack of verbal expression to a 1960s-driven fear of being seen as uncool by your kids and you have the perfect storm of awkward silence. You dig? The issue is not really that our kids don't want to talk, or know how. It's that *we* don't.

However, if your child were drowning, would you worry about how well *you* can swim or whether you're suitably dressed to execute a stylish rescue? No. You would jump in the water.

So, my advice is this: **Get past all of your own insecurities and lack of preparedness. Your kids need you**. *Jump in the water.*

And don't treat them like some different kind of animal. Anyone who has worked with kids knows that the secret to a genuine connection is speaking to them like adults. Kids can smell condescension from the first word.

But what about younger kids? you might well ask. *Do they want to talk as well?*

When I first developed the 5000 Days Project, I put a lower limit of age 7 because that is when kids start to develop an inner life and move beyond the "kids say the cutest things" phase. I stood firm on this for quite a long time, but kept getting requests from parents to start their kids at younger and younger ages because the process was helping their older brothers and sisters so much.

One day, I found myself welcoming a 4-year-old— a little Muslim boy—to the interview. I was thinking to myself, *What are you thinking, Rick? Is this really going to be worth my time and child's time?*

Well, upon sitting down I could see that he had a dark expression on his face. I asked him what was up. He told me that the girl he had planned to marry no longer wanted to marry him. I asked him how he knew. He replied that she had come up to him on the playground, pushed him down and declared that she no longer wanted to marry him. I told him that her messaging seemed pretty clear. But then I sat and marveled how this young boy processed his pain of rejection as well as I had ever processed any of mine. At the end he suddenly brightened up and declared, "But there is this other girl!"

I decided then and there that all kids at all ages want and need to talk. Are we ready to listen?

The Takeaway

What You've Forgotten About Being a Kid: More often than not, you'd really like to talk to somebody about what's going on in your life... but you don't really know how to do it very well, and it doesn't seem like your parents know how, either, *or* want to.

What You Can Do About That as an Adult: Work on your own communication. If you're not good at it yourself, there's only one way you're going to get better and be a good model for your kids, and that's to put on your big-kid pants, and get in the ring. Go out on a limb. Jump in the water. Your kids need you, and they need you to be the adult.

Family Matters

21 Things You Forgot About Being a Kid

Even though your family can embarrass you—and at times you may even hate them—underneath it all they are more important to you than anything else.

MY FINAL QUESTION OF each interview is, "What are you most grateful for?" I ask this in an attempt to send each child off in gratitude for the life they just reviewed. The answer to that question is 95% predictable.

They are grateful for *family*.

Obviously, many kids have wonderful families who fully deserve this adoration. But many do not.

In a future chapter, you will hear about Cristian, a Mexican immigrant whose father promised to follow his wife and three kids to the states. That was over a decade ago. He never showed. As a result, Cristian has had to grow up without a father. Despite this letdown, what is he nonetheless most grateful for? Family.

You will also hear about Simon, whose model family fell apart due to verbal abuse and infidelity. Family had been the foundation of Simon's life and its disintegration hit him hard, sending him down a path of personal destruction that usually kills nine out of ten people. Yet what is he most grateful for? Family.

Dazie's father was a First Responder and suffered from witnessing one too many tragic experiences, resulting in Post-Traumatic Stress Disorder. Dazie become the focus of his uncontrolled anger. She herself responded by violently lashing out at her mother, younger sister, *and* father. The home became a war zone as the family fell apart. Dazie developed an opioid addiction and struggled with her own mental health. Still, rebuilding her family through personal healing and forgiveness after a decade of pain remains her highest priority and the thing for which she is most grateful.

Several years ago, the 5000 Days Project was invited to Cambodia by two visionary women: Geraldine Cox, an Australian who founded the Sunrise orphanages, and her friend Mary-Anne Hatch, whom I mentioned in Lesson 2. The first time I saw one of the Sunrise orphanages in Siem Reap, I saw it from a roof top, sticking out among the grayish compounds because of its vibrant orange colors and the sound of musical instruments lofting from its walls. The orphanage next door with its dour walls and lack of laughter looked Dickensian next to Geraldine's creation.

At one point, Geraldine was criticized for spending money on music, drama, sport—things beyond the bare necessities. Her reply? "Wouldn't you spend that money on *your* kids?" When Mary-Anne heard about the 5000 Days Project, she approached me and made the case that orphans deserved the chance to grow their emotional intelligence as much as any other kid. Obviously, most of the kids were there because of some traumatic event and, in a country without many social services, Mary-Anne's appeal was an obvious opportunity to help.

Now, almost a decade later, one of "my kids" in the Cambodia 5000 Days project is Neath. She was sold by her mother to a Thai gang at age 3 for $50 and put to work as a beggar. She did not eat unless she brought in enough to "earn her keep." Neath was eventually taken off the streets and brought to Sunrise Orphanage. Her mother never came to claim her.

When **Neath** was age 5, officials thought it best to tell her that her mother had died. That night, she ran away from Sunrise and went looking for her mother. After an exhaustive search, two days later Neath was found sleeping on an anonymous grave several miles away.

Neath was 11 when she joined The 5000 Days Project. Her years at Sunrise had served her well though her missing mother had remained the emotional center of her life. She loved her more than anything and it did not seem to matter that she had been sold or abandoned.

Like lots of kids who come from traumatic backgrounds, Neath had a tendency to be bossy in an effort to control her chaotic world and, as a result, claimed to have "twenty enemies and only fifteen friends." Despite being an older sister to an admiring posse of younger orphan boys, she had difficulties with girls her own age. One kept pointing out that her mother had abandoned her, and this deeply upset her. I asked Neath if it was possible that her mother thought she'd be better off at Sunrise than on the streets, and she said she thought so.

By the time of her 12-year-old interview, Neath had succeeded in becoming less bossy and had vastly expanded her group of friends. She also had climbed to #19 in her class of 55. She was still struggling, however, with some kids looking down at her because of her lack of a parent. I asked Neath if her mother did prove to be still alive whether she would recognize her. She said no. I then asked what she would say to her. She said first she would hug her, and then she'd demand to know where she's been!

At age 13, Neath became the picture of poise and confidence. Her main problem was dealing with the constant attention of boys. She said that sometimes she had to take extreme measures: She would kick them, but then always apologized as she was walking away. It seems to work. However, for the boys, kicking seems to make their hearts grow fonder.

By 14, she had arrived at young womanhood with all of the emotions such a transition brings. The good news is that her world was now revolving around usual First World teen problems for girls—boys, friends, homework—which is a credit to Sunrise Orphanage. However, she could still be taken down by those who profess to being better than her because they have a family. The subject can destroy her.

In my most recent interview, I addressed that fear by helping **Neath** see the epic nature of her story and her heroic place in it. I challenged her to view her accomplishment of growing up without parents as a badge of honor rather than a scarlet letter. I told her that all of Western literature, starting with Charles Dickens, placed her at the center of a hero's journey. Sure enough, her strength, resilience and drive was a direct result of the challenges she has faced. She seemed to emerge from the interview a little taller but I still knew the greatest desire of her heart: To be with her mother, her only family.

■

ACROSS THE GLOBE, FAMILY stories include marital conflict, abuse, neglect, and even abandonment, as in the case of Neath. Thankfully, most family situations are not as extreme as Neath's. Still, I share it because even though the adult world has injured them or let down them down, nothing is as important to a child as family.

You will all remember seeing the hilarious notice on a neighborhood bulletin board that read something like:

HAVE YOU SEEN MY MISSING DOG?

Color: Dirt-brown. Splotchy skin.

Blind in one eye. Three legs.
Responds to the name Lucky.

No matter what condition our family is in, they are still the most important thing in the world to us. We love them. Even if we hate them. Even if they embarrass us. Even if they let us down. They are an essential part of who we are.

The Takeaway

What You've Forgotten About Being a Kid:
No matter what you might say otherwise, or how you might express your feelings about them—even if they have removed themselves from your life—nothing is as important to you as your family.

What You Can Do About That as an Adult:
Not much is more sad than people finally making peace with a family member at the point of death, and suddenly regretting the twenty years they spent letting egos get in their way. What a waste of life.

Try not to take a cold shoulder or insult to heart. See the larger picture and don't give power to the little things. And as your kids are figuring out their own place in the world, know that they are supposed to pull away and that sometimes that path of nature twists and turns in awkward and hurtful ways.

But there are always elastic bonds pulling your kids back. Rest assured that their hearts' desires lies with family. Afford them grace and you will both be blessed.

This does not mean you don't set boundaries against unhealthy behaviors or conflicting values. However, asking for and granting forgiveness, regardless how it is received, can be the best gift you will ever give yourself let alone give to others.

Judgment Day

21 Things You Forgot About Being a Kid

You feel constantly judged and know exactly where you are on the social ladder.

BY 2006 I WAS just over five years into The 5000 Days Project, and I visited a middle-school gym class to collect B-roll on one of the participants. The gym was filled with awkward sixth grade girls and boys putting forth enough energy to light a city.

When I arrived with my camera, there was the usual enthusiasm. "Are we going to be on the news?" "Will I be in a movie?" "Do you know Steven Spielberg?"

The one positive aspect of the increasingly stunted attention spans among youth is that, as a filmmaker, you can count on the buzz to last for all of five minutes before the kids grow bored with you and turn to something else.

Except this day.

There was one kid—gangly, thick glasses, with stringy hair part of which was dyed blue—who did not let up. Every time I started to film my 5000 Days kid,

Blue-Hair would jump in front of the camera and shout, "Hi, Mom!" This was minimally funny the first two times, but he kept doing it and doing it... and doing it. I would smile and laugh because long ago I decided that getting a shot was not worth hurting some kid's feelings. But I only had twenty-five minutes, and as the time dwindled down and this boy's desperate behavior continued, I realized the trip was likely going to be a total loss.

So... if he wanted attention, why not give him what he wanted? Maybe that would then free me to do my work.

As I turned the camera directly on him, he froze. "What are you doing?" he asked. I replied, "I'm filming you." He looked at me suspiciously, "Why?" Grasping at straws I replied, "Because you're interesting?" Suddenly, his cover dropped and the sweetest most vulnerable expression came on his face. He asked meekly, "Really?" Of course, the seriously annoyed part of me was thinking "No." However, I was in too deep so I offered to audition him for the project.

Three weeks later I interviewed him and found him to be one of the deepest, sweetest, most thoughtful kids I had ever interviewed. He lived alone with his equally amazing little sister and their caring, divorced dad—a bohemian artist who built exhibits at the Woodland Park Zoo. Here I had totally unfairly judged this kid and was ready to write him off. I would have missed not only an amazing story but making a good friend. **Zoriah** was used to getting ignored, dismissed, or criticized. That is part of every kid's world, and more so than usual in his case. I was so glad that an accident of circumstance led me to really pay attention.

This is, of course, a "don't judge a book by its cover" story, serving to remind me how deeply ingrained our instinct to judge is.

Theory of Mind is the field of Psychology's name for the unique human ability to read another person's physical and verbal cues, an ability which evolved from the need to assess danger and build alliances for survival. You need to know whether the person across from you represents a threat to your safety.

While the dangers are not as mortal as they once might have been, we still employ this skill for social advantage and emotional protection. Whether we like it or not, we are constantly judging other people by any number of factors, including physical appearance, speech, behaviors, clothes, the company they keep, the cars they drive. Hair color. Glasses. Video-bombing. Such judgment is instinctive, and is not meant to be cruel though often it comes off and can be used that way.

From their earliest interviews, most kids seem well aware of where they are on the social scale and where they fit into the pack. This grows much more intense as they approach teen years, at which point the awareness can become paralyzing.

One teen recently broke down the categories for me in her own school: braniacs, sporty types, popular kids and wannabe hangers-on, gamer boys, drama club (includes LGBT), popular rich Asians, nerds, emos, rappers, dazers (smokers), and so on. Social anxiety has never been greater among teens as the magnifying glass of social media makes the scrutiny and judgment even that much more intense.

During one of my own more self-conscious teen stages my dad would say, "Rick, you would not worry so much about what other people think of you if you knew how seldom they do." He was, of course, right. Most of us spend a lot more time worrying about ourselves than thinking about others. Still, judgment feels omnipresent whether it is based on parental or teacher assessments or the constant exposure to peers. And we learn to play both ends of it, alternately conforming when that is useful, and *refusing* to conform if that is *more* useful, as with Zoriah.

The more I ask questions about feelings of judgment the more I realize that this is primarily an issue of projection. Just as you often criticize in others that very thing you are most guilty of yourself, judgment works the same way. Nowhere is this more obvious than surrounding standards. Regardless of where you are on the "square vs. partier" spectrum, you tend to feel that those who are looser with their standards are making you feel too straight or uncool, while those who are straighter than you are tend to make you feel like a sinner! Naturally, though, no one can *make* you feel anything that you don't first feel yourself. Typically, the most judgmental person is the one looking back at you from the mirror.

Given this dilemma, I suggest to kids that they leave their judgment at the door. Yes, they'll need some of it for survival and to make quick survival decisions, but mostly it works to drag everyone down—especially the person doing the judging. They (we) tend to be its biggest victim. When they (we) feel paralyzed or victimized by it from others, I suggest they (we) examine their source of self-worth. (See Lesson 6!)

The Takeaway

What You've Forgotten About Being a Kid:
Even if you'd like to pretend otherwise, you are always keenly aware of where you stand on the social ladder—of how you are being judged for every one of your supposed faults or failures to somehow "measure up."

What You Can Do About That as an Adult:
Watch how your kids are dealing with social pressure, and their tendencies to either over-conform or rebel. Ask questions about how they are feeling judged for their appearance, values, or choices. Then just listen. Try not to "fix" things for them. And above all, don't become one of the primary sources of judgment!

The Anatomy of Self-Esteem

21 Things You Forgot About Being a Kid

Your friends, grades, sports, talents, and family define who you are and how you feel about yourself.

GRADES. FRIENDS. SPORTS/ARTS. FAMILY. When I ask young people where their self-worth comes from— their source of confidence and self-esteem—these are the Big Four answers. Grades. Friends. Sports/Arts. Family. After all, good grades, popularity, and athletic achievement are all rewarded from the moment we start school. Why shouldn't these areas be the ultimate source of self-worth? But *if* they are, why do even the highest achievers *still suffer so much self-doubt?*

Witness Emily. I started **Emily** in Grade Six and she was the ultimate achiever. Stellar grades, competitive at athletics, high-achieving parents and well-liked among

her friends. Despite all of this, she had a void in her that could not be filled.

Of all people, Emily deserved happiness and fulfillment. She worked harder than any other kid and refused to give up. She received accolades for her accomplishments, but the joy and satisfaction was always short-lived.

Now, I had this gifted, baby-faced friend in college named Greg Hickman who was 6'8" and one of the funniest people I knew. He used to do this thing when playing basketball that would put us all in stitches. He would reach down to pick up the ball only to have his huge foot kick it just beyond his grasp. Each time he would to this, it would get funnier and funnier. As a basketball player, it was his version of pursuing a moving goal line.

This was also Emily's story, though the result was not the least bit funny. She would achieve one amazing feat after another, but satisfaction always remained just beyond her reach. She, too, was chasing a moving goal line.

■

THIS STORY IS FAMILIAR to me because it is my story as well. I was not unlike Emily. I grew up with loads of friends in an upper middle class household with a supportive family. While I was not brilliant, I worked hard and got good grades. I was the lead singer in a rock band. I was decent athlete. I was an achiever. A perennial School or Class President.

My father worked like the dad in *Mary Poppins* except that instead of being a buffoon, he was so extraordinary that everybody wanted a piece of him. When we got him, he was the best father in the world. The problem was that we didn't get him enough, and I'm sure now that I became an achiever for that very reason. To get his attention. I was convinced that achievement would fill my void.

Achievement became my thing. With a lot of luck and circumstance but also hard work, I made it into Whitman, a prestigious private college, where I graduated in just over three years after having spent much of my Junior Year working for Senator Scoop Jackson in Washington, DC. From there, it was just a hop, skip, and a name-drop or two into the London School of Economics where I squeaked by getting my Master's Degree in International Relations.

Next stop? A doctorate at Oxford University with the goal of serving in the State Department as a career diplomat. I would study U.S.-Soviet relations under Professor Hedley Bull, perhaps the world's leading authority on my subject.

At Oxford, the road to a doctorate is very different from the American system. In the United States, doctoral candidates generally take classes, teach classes, take tests, and write their thesis in close association with the same supervisors who eventually determine their fate. At Oxford, you do not have to do any of that. You simply have to write a publishable book and pass your *viva* (Latin for "discussion").

The catch? The Viva is conducted by two outside examiners with no investment in you—examiners who hold your entire fate in their hands. As a result, the failure rate is much higher than it is Stateside, and breaks down into one of three categories if you do not pass: you are either "referred" (which means that you have to rewrite your book); you are offered a Master's Degree (a supreme insult for someone spending the usual 3-7 years in pursuit of a doctorate); or you are failed outright. While I was at Oxford, the latter actually happened to a former Vietnam General who had been writing his memoirs. Perhaps the examiners did not like the ending...

I was not about to let the opportunity go to waste. With so much self-directed time at my disposal I freely drank up all the "Oxford experience" had to offer.

My college had been founded in 1426 by Edward II and bordered the Christ Church Garden where a professor named Charles Dodgson, writing under the name Lewis Carroll, observed the Dean's daughter Alice frolicking through the flowers. Down the street was the pub where C.S. Lewis and J.R.R. Tolkien would meet weekly to dream up such works as *The Chronicles of*

Narnia and *The Lord of the Rings*. My roommate was an Etonian who would go on to produce one of the first viable hydrogen cars and whose acquaintances included Winston Churchill's grandson and Ian Fleming's nephew. During my first term, I took up rowing; and while on training runs around Christ Church meadow, I was shadowed by famed runner Roger Bannister's son.

I was aware that I was walking in the footsteps of greatness but instead of it being intimidating, I found it thrilling. My days concluded by researching my thesis in the Bodleian, the world's finest library. It was not a time for sleep. It was a time to live. And I had never felt so alive.

When Iranians seized the American Embassy in Tehran, I leveraged my International Relations emphasis into a gig with the Associated Press, eventually landing a plum assignment as Peter Jennings' assistant at ABC News in London. That, too, was thrilling, but it soon became clear to me that journalism was simply another form of entertainment. When I caught the movie bug and decided to become a filmmaker, I remember thinking, "If I'm going to do something superficial, I might as well make movies."

One of my Oxford tutors, Professor Michael Howard, knew David Putnam, who had just won the Oscar for *Chariots of Fire*, and John Schlesinger, who had done the same a few years before with *Midnight Cowboy*. Upon contact, they kindly consented to help, and I pulled a drinks party together consisting of some wealthy friends. That night we raised 10K pounds Sterling toward making our movie. The next morning, half of it was cancelled, of course, as people sobered up; but we had our start and the rest soon followed. I have already mentioned *Privileged*, which starred my fellow student Hugh Grant.

With the film receiving a premier at the prestigious British Film Institute and earning more money at the box office in Oxford than Spielberg's *E.T.*, it was time for me to get serious about a career. Accordingly, I accelerated work on my thesis and worked hard to complete it in two years instead of the usual three to seven. I did so with the blessing of Professor Bull, who sent it to his publishers at MacMillan. They promptly made an offer to bring it to market. I made plans for my graduation, my parents bought their plane tickets to be there for the ceremony, and the future looked sweet. All that remained was passing my Viva and receiving my doctorate.

Again, the Viva is effectively your verbal test on your thesis. On the appointed day, you dress up in suit, gown and white bow tie and make your way to the intimidating, marble-clad examination halls. Once there, your footsteps echo loudly on the marble floors as you go to a small door that is guarded by a small formally-dressed man. He nods and announces you. You the go through the small door to a long, narrow room with a chair in the middle and two silhouettes against the distant window.

After three hours' grilling I received the immediate verdict. "Mr. Stevenson, we will not be giving you your doctorate this year. You have at least another year of work to do. We are *referring* you."

I sat in stunned silence. This was not supposed to be part of the plan. I had a bright future to attend to. My parents already had their plane tickets. *I was already developing my next film.*

I walked back to my room and collapsed on my bed. I was devastated. After a lifetime of achievement, I had never faced a failure of this proportion.

I pretty much stayed in bed for two days, not knowing what to do, not wanting to call my parents. But then my phone rang. It was one of my newfound Oxford friends, David Young. On this day, he invited me to his office suggesting we talk. I told him I was not quite up to it, but he insisted.

As we walked later that day, he told me a story that would change my life. He told me how he had attended top private schools in America and had graduated at the head of his classes at Wheaton and Cornell Law School. He told me how he had married the most wonderful woman, had been recruited by one of New York's top law firms, and by age 29 had become special counsel to the White House Special Investigations Unit. There, he had a part in ordering the Watergate break-in. Due to a grave misjudgment on his part about the definition of loyalty, he had broken the law, fallen from grace with the rest of the Nixon administration, leaving the country he loved as a pariah in a plea-bargain over Watergate.

In the wake of this disaster, a good friend of his had shared with him the poem "If" by Rudyard Kipling—a poem that Kipling wrote to his son on how to be a man in the best sense of the word. One of the lines in the poem applied directly to him… and now me. It read, "If you can meet with Triumph and Disaster and treat those two impostors just the same… you'll be a man." I looked at him confused. He went on to explain, "'Triumph and disaster' are the successes and failures in your life. But that is all they are. They're simply a product of what you do, not who you are."

David continued. "I was not used to failure. I had based my self-worth on my successes. As a result, when failure came, it was devastating. Rick, your future field, show business, is full of people who base their self-worth on what they do versus who they are… and the result is that when they're on top, they're unbearable; and when they are on the bottom, they're suicidal. Is that the way you want to live?"

He concluded by saying, "This is your test to discover who you are. Are you humble, or are you all ego? Do you have faith in who you are or are you going to let yourself be defined by the judgment of two men you just met? Are you resilient and committed or are you a quitter?"

I realized that my entire life had been based on being an achiever, but that I was no closer to reaching any type of satisfaction than I was when I started.

I took a metaphoric deep breath and decided I wasn't going to quit. I would commit another year and do what it took. I called my parents, who were, of course, understanding and loving. And I went back to work. And I worked. I worked until my professor said that my thesis was the best work on détente that he had ever read. He told me I was ready.

A year later I walked into those examination halls, hearing the echo of my footsteps, hearing my name announced by the little man outside of the tiny door. With confidence, I proceeded into the room with the same two examiners. They pressed me for another three hours and at the end, they uttered a phrase that was so devastating that I can scarcely repeat it. They said, "Mr. Stevenson, we're not going to give you a doctorate. We're going to give you a Master's Degree."

I looked at them stunned. Did I hear them right? A Master's Degree? I already had a Master's Degree, and now I had put in three years—for nothing? I walked back to my room and once again collapsed on my bed. I stared at the ceiling for another three days. This was not the way my fairy tale was supposed to end.

I had learned my lesson, I thought. I had done the work. I had done the right thing and kept the faith.

Before long, though, the thought dawned: If I had *really* learned my lesson, I would not be letting myself be defined by this. I had done the work, learned what I needed to learn, and simply getting the degree was an ego thing, a formality. I called my parents, and they were understanding and loving, of course. And I took another deep breath and asked myself what a filmmaker would do with a doctorate anyway. Maybe get a better seat at a restaurant and be looked upon dubiously by other creative types? I had to laugh.

Just then my phone rang. Professor Bull was on the other end. He told me that he was so angered by the decision that he took the issue to the University-wide committee and, to his knowledge, for the first time in the 800-year history of Oxford University, I was being allowed to rewrite the thesis a third time, assuming that is what I wanted to do. He said that he felt I had gotten caught up in some academic politics and that I definitely deserved the degree.

Needless to say, I was stunned. I said, "Thank you," but I felt like putting a question mark on the end. "Thank you?" I was moved that he had stood up for me at some political cost to himself; but did I really want to do this again?

I rewrote once more, got my doctorate, and proceeded to never use it in the film business or even to get a table at a restaurant. I published my book through MacMillan—who, ironically, had me edit out many of the things the examiners had asked me to add. I don't really know the full truth of what happened but I do know that this "failure" changed my life for the better, getting me off the endless treadmill of achievement and leading me to base my self-worth on who I was versus what I did.

■

THANKS TO THIS EXPERIENCE, I now ask all 5000 Days Project kids an all-important question about their best personal character traits. Are they kind, empathetic, loyal, hardworking, resilient—which traits can they claim? And once they claim them and see what they're made of, I let them know that they have found the source of their self-worth. All of those external factors—grades, friends, sports, family—are just products of what they *do* but don't define who they are.

That is, unless they *let* those things define who they are.

If they do, they are giving away their power, outsourcing it to others, begging for the approval of most-likely irrelevant examiners. If you base your self-worth in what others think of you, a bad look from a friend or a family member can be devastating... but it may in reality have nothing to do with you. It may just be indigestion.

A bad grade just means you need to work harder.

And if you're not failing at least some of the time, it means you are not challenging yourself enough. That's all.

The good thing about the source of self-worth is in the title. It can only come from within—from yourself. And that is something that no one can take away from you.

■

BACK TO **EMILY**. SHE did have some Senior Year setbacks—not getting Head Girl and not getting into her first choice of universities. After commiserating, I asked her if she really needed another accolade to discover how amazing she already is. Her reply? A smile revealing a new-found wisdom. Hopefully, these "failures" will be steps to her learning how to deal with the "triumphs and disasters" in life.

The Takeaway

What You've Forgotten About Being a Kid: You might know better, but you still find that friends, grades, sports, talents, and family define who you are and how you feel about yourself.

You are most likely either driven to achieve, or self-sabotaged by fear of failure.

What You Can Do About That as an Adult:
The process of helping kids redefine "success" and "failure" is a long, hard road but one upon which hyper-achievers and "underachievers" alike can be set free. Start by looking at your own life, and the ways in which you have taught your kids to measure themselves. Share your own failures. Those failures may prove to be the biggest gift you can give them.

Lesson 7

Buckle Up!

21 Things You Forgot About Being a Kid

Whether you show it or not, your emotional life is a rollercoaster. You feel the highest highs and lowest lows. Even the little things are big.

UP TO AGE 13, I had quite a temper. Labeled as a "sensitive boy," **I lived up to that description** by getting alternatively very upset or very happy and everything in between. My mother always attributed it to three things. First, she theorized that I "inherited" my temper from my father's father who, according to her, was passed over for many promotions at work for expressing his feelings at the wrong time. I'm not sure you can inherit a temper but my paternal grandfather, despite being a good grandfather, was consistently held out as an example of "inappropriate expressions of emotion."

Second, my "artistic temperament" was attributed to my interest in music, drama, and other creative things. I would spend hours playing a story game with friends called "Adventure" in our yard. The swing set was a sailing ship, the five tall Douglas fir trees were a forest, our plastic baseball bats were swords. Long play-filled days were spent making up adventures while getting shot or stabbed as many times as possible. I'm not sure what that was all about but death by imaginary gunshot occurred almost hourly. Not long after, Clint Eastwood's character Josey Wales would say, "Dyin' ain't much of a living"—but it was for us.

Finally, my temper was attributed to my delayed development. Despite being tall, I had a late birthday and I had been set back by being deaf for most of my 3rd year of life. Yes, deaf. My mother and father noticed I was not responding to their calls and had my hearing tested. Sure enough, I had lost my hearing. For several months, they could not find an explanation until finally, after my tonsils were removed, my hearing magically came back. Still, I had lost a vital year of speech development and entered Kindergarten on the "extremely immature" side.

One day during my 13th year, however, I lost my temper—not as in "*losing* losing" my temper but in terms of it going away altogether.

I was the leader of a rock band that had been hired to play several gigs around the community. We had four members and the youngest one was Craig, who had the unfortunate combination of being twice as talented and twice as immature as everyone else in the band. We would be playing a gig and he would suddenly decide he didn't want to play a specific song. The audience would look on as we argued over what song to play next.

One day we were practicing in my basement which had the 1970s low ceilings and Craig pulled one of his stunts. Furious, I jumped up from my keyboards saying "Enough!" and managed to crack my head on the ceiling. Everyone went silent for a moment then burst out laughing. While it was funny, I was fuming not only from my sore head but from my anger toward Craig. I said, "Forget it!" and stormed out of the house, walking down the middle of the street talking to myself like some crazy man. I had never been so angry.

About a quarter of a mile away from the house, I suddenly stopped and thought, "Wait, why did *I* leave? That's *my* house!" As I turned right around and started to march back, it occurred to me that my mother had been right all along. This "temper thing" was not working. I vowed from that moment on never to lose my temper again. And with rare exceptions, I have not done so to this day.

This had two effects. The plus side for me was that at a time when my friends were growing more irritable and volatile due to puberty, I somehow managed to be the smooth sailor, the steady, rational one in a sea of pubescent emotion. I generally made wise decisions, had a good relationship with my parents and teachers, and was chosen to lead from student body office to sports, scouts, and arts.

The downside, which I would not discover until much later, was that these social skills came at a cost. I was still getting angry. I was just unwilling to let myself *express* the anger. In fact, I was afraid of my own anger. I didn't like myself when angry. It made me ugly. The thing about emotions, however, is that they are what they are. You can deny them but they're still there trying to reveal some truth to you if you are willing to listen. If you are not willing to listen, they can express themselves physiologically through headaches or other "pain" spots.

Five years into starting The 5000 Days Project, I started getting three migraine headaches a week. I tried all of the medicines and even went through various procedures to rid myself of the pain. One medication worked but none of the procedures made a lasting difference. Ten years after trying everything legal, my counselor, Donna, asked me if I heard a lot of painful things during these interviews. I told her yes, unbelievably painful things. She asked what I did with the pain. I told her that for the first five years I would come home and cry. It seemed really unfair that these kids had to experience what they were experiencing. I had never had to experience pain like that. She nodded and then asked me again what I did with the pain. I told her that about five years in I decided that the fact the kids were able to exorcise their feelings in their 5000 Days interview was a good thing and it gave me hope for them. Time and time again I saw the unveiling of these emotions release the individual to live in a healthier state. Donna then asked me a third time what I did with the pain. A bit impatient I replied, "What do you mean, what did I do with the pain?" She shrugged and said, "How do you process it? It goes in—but if nothing is done with it, it doesn't go away. It just sits there and eats you like a cancer."

Classic. Despite me advising everyone else to exorcise their pain, I was doing nothing with my own— the pain that came from hearing all of these stories and feeling for all of these kids. I just shook my head. Was I still that deaf and blind? Of course, that was a significant part of the problem. While part of my problem was physiological (my AA joint), my physical pain was dramatically exacerbated by my inability to process the external input I was receiving. Donna got me going on some mindfulness. I learned to acknowledge the pain, hold it, feel it, then release it. Within three weeks, my migraines had been reduced to one per week. Never again would I doubt the connection between our mental health and our physical health.

Over my 5500+ interviews, I have seen kids attempt to handle their pain in a wide variety of ways. Kids deflect with humor or punish others (the basis of bullying). Some kids develop an addiction to video games because it's an escape from reality. As teens they may take up drinking, drugs, sex, or any of the adult methods of pain relief.

But before all of that, I see something happen in each and every one of us that is much more subtle and more "acceptable" than the vices. We develop what I call the "music equalizer effect." An equalizer is that multi-slider deck in a music studio which controls the entire range of frequencies in music. It can be used to take off the low end of a song so that it does not destroy your woofers and/or the high end of a song so that it does not break the glasses in your house. It creates a type of audio safe-zone.

Likewise, as we grow and get slapped if not hit with the harsher side of human relationships and outright circumstance, we start to develop our own emotional safe-zone—which begins to narrow our available range of happiness and sadness. A classic example is a break up. Someone hurts us and we naturally raise more defenses and walls to protect ourselves from that happening again.

Now, the good thing about the "music equalizer effect" is that it protects our speakers and fine stemware. The bad thing is that we don't hear the full beauty of the music!

I see this time and time again in kids as they grow. The more sensitive ones pay the price and tend to shut down earlier. In adulthood, such a person may appear to you to be a pessimist or a cynic. But as my favorite phrase goes, "A cynic is just an idealist with one too many disappointments."

Consider puberty, which is nature giving us a hypodermic needle-sized dose of mind- and body-altering drugs. Why do teens develop an interest in sex? Not because they are sinners, but because nature has just given them a loading dose of something akin to Viagra. Why do they start questioning everything their parents do? Because nature is telling them it's time to start separating and leaving home.

By the time we're adults, we've settled into a routine of predictability. We get educated, earn money, and build walls to avoid "the slings and arrows of outrageous fortune," to defend ourselves against the unpredictable. The unknown. We spend *years* earning this—molding the environment to our liking even if it is just our own easy chair in front of the TV.

Kids have no such luxury. Not only do they have volcanic changes going on inside their bodies throwing them constant curveballs, but they also face a jungle of uncertainty absolutely every day at school surrounded by their fellow crazies. It truly is a wonder we survive. The question is, at what cost?

Every kid I've ever interviewed is of course somewhere on the spectrum of emotional bandwidth restriction per the music equalizer effect; the challenge is helping them become aware of the consequences of their level of emotional protection. Obviously, those kids who keep themselves wide open can become the canary in the coalmine, the first to keel over due to their own vulnerability. Those who shut themselves down lose empathy and the ability to love for fear of loss.

With all of our emotions based in our fears or our desires, our goal should be to help kids *and* ourselves develop emotional intelligence to the point where we can identify, hold and process all that happens to us while remaining open enough to love big, trust big and experience the full beauty of the music.

The Takeaway

What You've Forgotten About Being a Kid:
The feelings are all there—the peaks and the valleys! Over time, your goal becomes not to *keep* feeling, but to tame the rollercoaster. This helps you feel more under control... but at what cost?

What You Can Do About That as an Adult:
Start by learning how to process your own emotions in a healthy way. Then you can model the process for your kids. The goal is to help you *and* them experience the full range of

feelings, eventually becoming masters of your emotions rather than victims.

Lesson 8
Fears for Tears

21 Things You Forgot About Being a Kid

Crying is *not* cool.

IT JUST SUDDENLY HAPPENS. Your eyes well up and despite your efforts to suppress or hide it, here it comes. That tear rolling down your cheek making you feel vulnerable, like you're a little baby. Can you imagine anything worse? The show of weakness? The ugly expression. The pure humiliation?

But there *is* something worse. *Not* doing it.

Theorists postulate two explanations for *h. sapiens'* triumph on the Savannah over other animals:

- The size of our brains.
- Our unique ability to perspire.

Intelligence is one thing—but it's sweating, the body's means of cooling itself, that enabled us to stalk and track an animal past the latter's point of exhaustion.

■

HE SAT ACROSS FROM me, 10 years old, looking stoic. This was indeed a strange experience for both of us—him speaking Khmer through an interpreter to some inquisitive American many years his senior.

His mother had died in childbirth. Brokenhearted and resentful, the boy's father had abandoned him at the Siem Reap Sunrise Orphanage. Again The 5000 Days Project had been invited to the Sunrise Orphanages in hopes that it might help to nourish the emotional health of these children who had been through so much.

Sophea was not suspicious. He was more taken back that someone was actually interested in asking how he was. In a country that lost an entire generation to genocide, the question "How are you?" is rarely asked and is considered luxuriously indulgent. Furthermore, sharing one's feelings, as healthy as it might be, runs against some cultural norms.

As the relationship grew over the next few years, the interviews went deeper and the boy began to open up. But I knew the clock was ticking. Age 14 is when the weapons of emotional protection are fully deployed as boys try to figure out what it means to be a man. This boy was no different except for the fact that Sunrise had recently discovered the whereabouts of his father. He had been working on a farm nearby all along and had never come to visit.

When I asked him about it, he told me that his dad was just busy. I dug deeper. Even on a holiday, why had his father not come to visit? The boy shrugged but I could see a world of emotion building in his face. When I asked a third time, including how he felt about that, the dams suddenly broke. He cried. His entire body shook as a lifetime of pent-up emotion poured out of him. He continued to cry as we explored the sadness and disappointment he felt over having an absentee father and never having known the feeling of being held by his mother. Mary-Anne and I stood and put our arms around him as he grieved.

Thanks to the caring of the Sunrise staff and this emotional awakening, the next year the boy had a lightness about him that was evident in everything he did. He actually had gone to see his father, and had come to terms with who he was and who he wasn't. Sunrise helped him get a job in the tourist industry so his ability with English had grown dramatically, and now, **at age 18, Sophea** was excited to be doing our interview without an interpreter. He told me that he visited his now-aging and ailing father weekly, and had become the son he'd

always wanted to be. Confident, happy, and enthusiastic, after this emotional vetting he had decided to define himself rather than let circumstances define things *for* him.

■

HAVING SEEN KIDS TEAR up more times than not in my thousands of interviews, I believe that crying might be the body's emotional equivalent of sweating—acting as a cooling system, a stress regulator, and especially a means of releasing emotional toxins. In fact, Dr. William Frey, a biochemist at the Ramsey Medical Center in Minneapolis, has found that different tears have different chemical makeup. For tears of emotion shed stress hormones thereby giving us relief.

Another vital benefit of crying involves what we can learn from it. With a few key questions, I can usually identify what a child *needs* to talk about because while we are well practiced in lying and/or denial when it comes to avoiding painful topics, our expressions don't lie. If it's true that our eyes are the windows to our soul, we should not be surprised that our tears are shed from those windows.

Case in point: I recently conducted Year Six of my interviews with a Canadian girl who had come from a happy, functional, and highly-successful family. She was a competitive athlete, never had any crises to share, and had never shed a tear in any interview. Now, at age 17, she was about to enter her Senior Year with university on the horizon.

Over the previous two interviews, the biggest struggle she had shared involved her grades. She was at a private school where, the previous year, 100% of the students had been placed in some institution of higher learning—in many cases, the finest universities in North America and Europe. She had shared that she did not feel very smart and hence did not speak up much in class. Her grades were in the low-B, high-C level.

Whenever a student expresses the feeling that they're not very smart, I explore the feeling with them because many fall back on that feeling as their primary narrative and it becomes a self-fulfilling prophecy. The reasons are almost always based in a deeper fear.

As we started to talk about choices of university, she started to tear up for the first time. I asked her what was going on. She just shook her head, unused to and uncomfortable with this reaction. In fact, she had told me before that moment that she could not remember the last time she had cried. I asked her if she was prepared to dig a bit deeper. She nodded, cautiously. I asked her, "Is this about competition? About getting into a place on par with your friends?" She shrugged. I continued, "Is it about not knowing what your future holds and feeling uncomfortable with the challenges ahead?" She considered this and gave a partial nod but then a shrug.

"Wait. Is this about not even wanting to go to university?" She looked up in fear, then burst out into full-fledged tears. "Everyone assumes I'm going but I don't even *want* to go. I have *never* wanted to go. But *no one ever asked me*." She had never said any of this aloud— even to herself. Her tears had told the truth.

I will profess a bias for any form of higher education even though a good argument can be made against its value and utility for a specific individual at present. With college costs and student debt ballooning and with no guarantee of a job upon completion, higher education does not provide the guarantees it did in previous times. I told her that not going to college was always an option and that many people had been successful without it. But I also told her she needed to explore her own feelings surrounding it so that she was making a fully-informed decision.

Over a tearful twenty minutes, she described how miserable she had been in her classes, always feeling like the stupid one. As we explored her feelings about college, we discovered that her reluctance was more about repeating that feeling of insufficiency over the next four years than about the actual university experience. Wow. What a vital piece of self-knowledge. Sadly, she had also been unable to explore this due to her fear of disappointing her parents.

I know her parents and I knew that they will be supportive of this discussion. In fact, it will bring them all closer at a vital time. Because this happened so recently, the jury is still out but hopefully, whatever the decision, it will be the right one for her.

In this case and most others, tears might be considered vital clues running down our face—the body's involuntary lie-detector aided by gravity. These are truths that must be told.

I'm writing about this because we as adults often forget that each day growing up can involve the highest highs and the lowest lows, as we discussed in Lesson 7.

First, as kids, our brains have not yet fully developed and we don't have the life experience to deal with everything being thrown at us.

Second, during puberty, nature is injecting us with a cocktail of hormones we would not wish on a drug addict.

Third, a tsunami of information and input washes over us constantly and we have no time to process it.

Fourth, fear and division dominate our discourse and our politics. And we take it all in—and hold it in—only to have it threaten to eat away at us like a cancer.

My advice to kids and adults alike? Cry.

Forget the fear of looking ugly—cry.

Forget the fear of looking weak—cry.

As a father, I cry weekly—mostly out of happiness but sometimes the other.

So do this for yourself. Cry. Especially you guys. Get your tear ducts in order. Man up! Cry.

The Takeaway

What You've Forgotten About Being a Kid: One of the worst things you can ever do is show weakness through tears.

What You Can Do About That as an Adult: Work it out. Cry. And encourage your kids to cry! Our wellbeing depends on it.

The Art of Hating Math

21 Things You Forgot About Being a Kid

It is difficult to get motivated when you don't see the connection between what you're taught in school and your future.

"WHY DO I HAVE to take trigonometry? I want to be a landscape designer. I can't get motivated. I *hate* math."

Of all of the things I hear in interviews, this is one of the most common. Math is *usually* the target—but English, social sciences, and languages take pretty good hits as well depending on the interests or strengths/weaknesses of the child. And in many cases, this is a difficult question to answer. Why take languages if you are committed to being a scientist? Why learn military history if you are going to be a doctor?

My answer? "Drop it." The student looks shocked. "What?"

I enunciate for clarity, "Drop it. Drop math."

"Can I do that?" the student asks.

"Sure. I'm a big believer that you should never do what you don't want to do. Do you want to do math?" I probe.

"No," the student says. "But I need it for graduation. It's a requirement."

"Oh, you want to graduate?" I ask. The student nods.

"Why? Lots of people don't graduate."

"Well, I want to get into a good university" the student says.

"Why?" I ask. "Lot of people don't go to university."

"Well, I want to get into a good university so I can get a good job." the student says, starting to question this line of inquiry.

"And what's your definition of a 'good' job? There are plenty of jobs."

The student asserts, "A 'good' job is one that I will enjoy going to every day. I don't want to have a job I hate."

"Why?" I ask again.

The student becomes a bit annoyed, "Because I want to have a happy life."

"Okay," I say. "Now let's reverse engineer that. You want to have a happy life... which requires you having a job you love, which means going to a good university, which means getting *into* a good university, which requires graduating from school—which involves taking *math*.

"So... You *do* want to do math, after all?"

The student looks at me confusedly, then slowly

nods. This fact cannot be denied.

"And let me ask you another question. Currently, is your math homework ten times harder than your other homework because you hate it?" I ask.

"Yes. Absolutely."

"How would you like to make it ten times easier?"

Another nod, suspiciously.

"Your answer is simple. You may not think you like math but you have already decided you're going to do it because you want everything that comes from it.

"So you have two choices. You can hate it and continue feeling victimized; or you can try to find the love of it. As you know, there are at least two ways of looking at exactly the same thing. Because you are deciding not to make your peace with math, you make it ten times harder on yourself. Why would you possibly do that to yourself since you've already decided to take it? If you use your creativity to find the love of math, you not only make it ten times easier but you will learn how to turn things that victimize you into things you master."

■

OF COURSE, IT'S NEVER really *that* easy. This doesn't happen with a snap of the fingers. How do you "find the love" of something you don't inherently enjoy or find difficult?

A good and vital first step is finding the reasons

behind the feeling. For instance, my son, Oliver, "hated math" and was always in "catch-up mode." Math and languages are particularly difficult because when you get even a tiny bit behind, you feel like you're a *mile* behind. Oliver is a smart kid and, like most of us, does not like the things that make him feel otherwise. We got him a tutor and now miraculously, he is enjoying it. When he said he "hated math," it was never about the *math*, really; he hated *feeling stupid*.

We often say certain kids have a "head for math" or a "head for social sciences." Assuming some version of that is true, how do we find the love of something for which we don't "have a head"? The answer involves putting the question in a broader perspective. We need to look at the task as one of those "difficult things" that we will face in life; and if we can rewrite the challenge in our heads to rise above a particular difficult thing we will gain confidence in facing similar difficult things in the future.

In other words… punt on math now, and you'll probably punt plenty of other things later. Learn to love math now… and that experience may later help you save your job, your marriage, or your relationships with your kids! That could *really* make me love math.

Second, while the human brain can process about eleven million bits of information at a time, it can only consciously focus on forty to fifty of them. If most of those forty-odd thoughts filling up the conscious part of your mental hard drive are negative—if they're about how much you hate math—then that will be your reality and your burden.

A few years ago I was introduced to a revolutionary approach to my migraines. Evidently, most of the pain that creates a headache goes through the trigeminal nerve running across the center of your forehead. When a sufficient number of pain signals fill up that nerve, you have a headache.

A company called Cefaly theorized that if, before the onset of a headache, you can fill up that nerve with neutral messages, then there will be no room for the pain messages. Accordingly, it created a device that shoots neutral messages via neuro-stimulation into that nerve via a small electrical charger and a sticky pad. It has proven hugely effective in the world of migraine treatment.

If we apply the same theory to the forty or fifty thoughts that fill our mental hard-drives, can we consciously direct the thoughts we want to have in a way that is helpful to us? That is what all great athletes, performers and others call their "mind game."

Clearly, the way to "find the love" of something we don't automatically love is to up our mind game.

Oliver generally loves his teachers but there was one with whom he did not see eye to eye. He complained that that teacher was causing him to hate a subject he had previously loved. I pointed out to him that while the teacher could make the subject less fun for him, only one person can make him hate it—and that's Oliver.

My primary goal with adjusting perspectives is to help students realize that they have more control over things than they think. The world is split between people who see themselves as victims and people who work to become masters of each situation. It is all a mind game. Why not play it in your favor?

The Takeaway

What You've Forgotten About Being a Kid: A great many of the things we "have to do" seem completely pointless, with no connection to what we want from life.

What You Can Do About That as an Adult: Realize that you can *always* improve your mind game in every area of your life. The more you practice it, the more you model it for your kids. And the more you all become masters of your thoughts, instead of victims.

Attitude v. Gratitude

21 Things You Forgot About Being a Kid

School is a prison sentence... and the main reason you go is to see your fellow inmates.

BELLEVUE, WASHINGTON, DECEMBER 1941.

A 17-year-old boy is halfway through his Senior Year with plans to become an engineer. He wants nothing more than to build—bridges and buildings. As student body President and co-captain of the football team, he is positioned to get into a good university. And then suddenly, on the morning of December 7th, the Japanese attack Pearl Harbor and everything changes.

Every red-blooded boy in his class wants to go fight for his country. Sure enough, the next morning, most of the boys in the senior class are absent, having opted to go down to the recruitment center to sign up to fight. This boy does the same but is told that as a 17-year-old, he cannot not sign up without his parents' permission. Disappointed, he goes home and begs his parents to let him go.

Despite being great patriots, no parents want their children to go off to war. However, this boy's parents know that he is turning 18 within the next three months anyway. So, they pray about it and the next morning deliver their verdict. They will allow their son to make up his own mind as long as he speaks with Mr. Oglemeyer first. Now, Mr. Oglemeyer is the kind of teacher that hopefully all of us are lucky enough to have at least once in our lives—that teacher who cares about us and goes that extra mile. The boy agrees and goes to visit his mentor.

Mr. Oglemeyer listens carefully then shares his advice with the boy. He tells him that the war is going to be a long one, that there will be plenty of war for him to fight and that he will be of more use to his country if he finishes high school and starts one term at university before enlisting. He has a lot going for him and this will ensure that he will have something to come back to.

This is not the advice the boy wants to hear, but he so respects his teacher that he follows it—completing his Senior Year and attending one term at Washington State University before shipping out to war.

During that term at Washington State University that young man meets my mother. They eventually get engaged, and when he returns from war they both go into teaching. My father not only becomes one of the nation's youngest and most successful superintendents, but he goes on to hold a number of leadership positions on state and national education associations. Bridges and buildings can wait. He is going to build lives.

■

I TELL THIS STORY because the real superstars in our lives are not football quarterbacks or rock stars; they are teachers. Teaching is generally held up to be the most honorable of professions despite the lack of financial recognition.

There are of course bad teachers, mediocre teachers, and formerly good teachers who have simply burnt out. As in any profession, there is an entire range of quality. Should it be easier to remove bad or mediocre teachers? Absolutely, because the stakes are so high. However, teachers as a group have too often been unfairly targeted as the source of what is wrong with our education system. Since the majority of them are public employees and, in theory, "work for us," they can become targets for everything from our frustrations with government and taxes to our frustrations with our kids and ourselves. Depending upon our own experience with "school," they also catch all of our projections, good and bad, from that time. After all, we have *all* had teachers.

Recently I was on a phone call with a salesman who seemed intrigued by what I was doing. He wanted to know more so I told him about the positive experience I was having in schools. He responded by telling me about teachers in his home state of Texas who were manipulating the system to get double salaries. He claimed that they were just in it for the money. I was not sure how to respond. Of all things that can be legitimately thrown at teachers, "being in it for the money" was not one of them. Upon further inquiry, I discovered that his school days had not been good ones and that he held a lot of feelings (and prejudices) from that time. Now, in the present, he looks at his former "tormentors" who get three months off a year and a high personal satisfaction level from their jobs as what's wrong the educational system and America as a whole.

One of the privileges of doing The 5000 Days Project is that I've been allowed to see a whole range of educational models across the world. With few exceptions, I have marveled at the innovation, creativity, and commitment of those educators across the U.S., Canada, Australia, the U.K., and other developed countries. I am inspired and encouraged by their efforts in the face of endless testing, declining budgets, and rising danger as they continue to strive for excellence. I am sure I carry my own prejudices—but keeping the company of teachers, people who have chosen to give their lives to preparing and inspiring the next generation despite the lack of fame or fortune, is one of the honors of doing what I do.

In developing countries, however, excellence is not always the goal. On a recent trip to Cambodia, one of the kids from Sunrise Orphanage told me how she was not sure how she was going to pass her grade because she lacked the money to bribe her teacher. I was stunned.

"Bribe the teacher?"

"Yes," she said. "Teachers only make $30 per month at their school work so they have to make the rest of their money through bribes."

Later I asked Geraldine Cox, the founder of Sunrise, what the kids did in the face of this social pressure, and she said that Sunrise had enough kids in the system that the teachers did not typically "charge" them for grades… or else they would hear from her!

Despite this incident, the majority of teachers in developing countries are nothing short of heroic especially given their lack of resources and facilities. That said, they do have one often-overlooked advantage over their counterparts in the wealthier developed countries. And that advantage goes a long ways to make up for the disparities in facilities and resources.

This advantage is a game changer, and I can't overestimate the impact. We in the developed world have a lot to learn from it.

What is it?

Gratitude.

Unlike their colleagues in the developed work, these teachers get to lead a classroom full of kids who are, generally, grateful to be there.

Most students in developing countries see education as a privilege, and attend to their studies with commitment and enthusiasm. Despite the advantages of one hundred times the spending, the best teachers, and the most advanced innovation possible, students in developed countries view school as a prison sentence— time to be served. This became glaringly obvious as various schools in America, Canada, Australia, and the UK asked me to ask students about their favorite part of school. Sadly, *very* rarely does someone ever mention anything about academics, classes, teaching styles, or opportunities. The *favorite* part is almost always about getting to see friends.

When did this happen? When did we lose appreciation for this privilege called education? When did we take it all for granted? Even though I was raised by educators, the language in even our household was "You *have* to go to school," versus "You *get* to go to school."

Here is the bottom line, and why this is so significant: **Students who are grateful to be in school are many times more teachable than students who feels like they have to be there.** The proof is in the fact that immigrant students in developed countries who come from homes grateful for the opportunity consistently score higher than their jaded counterparts.

A related factor revolutionized my view of what is right and wrong with education. As my Brain Scientist friend/guru, John Medina, pointed out: "Contrary to popular belief, the brain actually had no interest in learning. It's a survival organ. What determines our interest in learning is our emotions, or what artists call 'the heart.' In this way, 'the heart' is actually the engine and 'the brain' is the carriage. What is wrong with our 19th Century model of education is that most schools have got that backwards."

When I was invited to bring the Project to Geelong Grammar School, one of Australia's leading private schools, I was astounded by the fact that just over a decade ago, they had done something extremely daring. Despite over a century of legendary success producing some of Australia's most successful people (and Prince Charles as well), they had decided to take a radical shift, prioritizing student wellness *above* academics with the goal of producing happier and more fulfilled, purpose-driven students. Over a decade later, their students are now performing better than ever because their emotional needs are being met. Through their Institute of Positive Education, Geelong is carrying this message to thousands of schools around the world.

Of course, Geelong Grammar School is not alone in this mission. Julie and I actually moved countries to enroll our two youngest kids in West Point Grey Academy in Vancouver, which operates under a similar philosophy. When kids' emotional needs are prioritized, everything else follows. With about one-third of the students at WPGA participating in The 5000 Days Project, it has been interesting to see what gratitude students have for being at the school.

Hoping to send kids out on the most positive note

possible, I conclude every interview with the question, "What are you most grateful for?" Again, the most common answer is "family" but the second most common answer with West Point Grey Academy kids, is "getting to attend this school." This if often followed by expressions about, "the 'privilege' of getting to grow up and learn in this environment" or "being given so many opportunities that other kids don't get." This culture of gratitude has been the result of visionary leadership, an engaged and well-trained faculty and staff, families who prioritize it, and a student body of kids who strive to practice it. Despite only being founded a quarter of a century ago, a recent study put West Point Grey Academy in the top tier of all Canadian schools. With a bit of research, you can find a few key schools—both public and private—across the developed world that have discovered and practice a similar approach.

I realize bringing gratitude back into the culture of a school, let alone a nation or the developed world, is a huge cultural shift. However, I am not sure if we as adults could do more for education than facilitating this shift. Thomas Jefferson saw education as essential to our very freedom. "Enlighten the people generally, and tyranny and oppressions of body and mind will vanish like evil spirits at the dawn of day."

Standing tallest among the American Founding Fathers and as an author of the Declaration of Independence, Jefferson believed in protecting the right to disagree but also the need to arm citizens with the education to separate fact from fiction. In an age of misinformation and "alternative facts," the need for education to work has never been greater.

The exciting thing is that each of us can have a part to play in facilitating this return to gratitude toward education. It starts with our own thought process and the language we use in our conversations with our kids.

Look at the shift in attitudes toward issues like gay marriage or gender equality in less than a decade. Such cultural transformations are possible. And the good news is that this shift does not cost us a penny.

It involves each and every one of us developing a new attitude toward gratitude.

We can start this way: With any luck, each of us have at least one special teacher or mentor if not several who have cared enough about us to go the extra mile. Remember and appreciate them. Mine include among others Mrs. Bates, Mr. Wills, Mr. Nichols, Ms. Sherick, Mr. Alderdice, Dr. Edwards, and Dr. Breit. They all shared two things in common. First, they demanded a lot from me and had high expectations. Second, they infused me with a love of learning.

Oh, and yes, I should mention Mr. Oglemeyer. Without his advice to my father, I would not be here, and you would no doubt be reading something much less redeeming!

Who were the teacher or teachers who made a difference in your life?

The Takeaway

What You've Forgotten About Being a Kid: School does not feel like a privilege; it feels like a prison, and you're just glad you like some of the inmates!

What You Can Do About That as an Adult: Start by checking your own attitudes and prejudices at the door. Reposition school as the opportunity it is. Change the language game, starting today. Kids who "get to" go to school will always do better than kids who "have to" go to school. Is it a mind game? Sure, every which way. So, be smart, play it in your child's favor. Your kids will be happier and better learners.

The Monster Under the Bed

You think your greatest fear is spiders...

AS A YOUNG, STRUGGLING screenwriter/director in the film business, the following realization significantly improved the way I wrote my characters: *We all live on a continuum between our longings and our fears. Where we are on that spectrum defines how we live our lives.*

Based on my interviews, I have confirmed that this is as true in life as it is in fiction. If you can figure out your greatest fear and greatest desire, you have figured out the majority of yourself.

Helping children identify their desires and longings is fairly straightforward. I ask about their dream job when they grow up, and their top three wishes. I ask what makes them happy and sometimes I have them play "Ideal Futures," where they describe their perfect life at age 35.

In the majority of cases, preteen children know what they want and are not afraid to dream: playing center forward for Barcelona, touring the world as a singer/songwriter, saving lives as a surgeon, writing bestselling novels. As they become teenagers and some dreams are disappointed or they become aware of the harsher realities of the world, one of two things happens.

First, they may refine their ambitions so that they become more reachable. For instance, a girl who had wanted to be in the WNBA might decide she wants to be a high school basketball coach. A boy who wanted to be a painter might want to work in visual effects or be a graphic designer.

Second, some kids may not make the transition. As a result, they become lost. Of course, it is perfectly fine to not know what you want to do at age 13. However, working to identify your passion provides a compass for your future. Without some direction, you risk losing yourself at sea and becoming a passenger on someone else's ship when the goal is to captain your own. In the end, how can you live the life you imagined if you never imagined the life you wanted to live?

So that's desires. Complicated, but not cryptic. On the flipside, however, most children don't have a clue about their fears. When asked what they are afraid of, 90% will say "Spiders." Having seen a BBC documentary on the love life of spiders, I happen to think spiders get a bad rap; but that's not the point. The point is that without understanding their deeper fears, kids risk becoming the victim of them. And spiders are really the least of their worries.

Let me give some examples.

■

WE ADOPTED MY DAUGHTER Leah at age 3. She had been taken by the state of Utah from a mother who suffered from alcoholism and had difficulty taking care of her daughter. Evidently, Leah had been in the car during a series of DUIs.

Our birth child, Oliver, was also 3 years old at the time and, despite an initial moment of bewilderment and jealousy, the two of them became inseparable. They became best friends. However, Leah was bossy—*very* bossy. This is common in children who have been neglected. They do everything possible to shape and control the unpredictable world around them.

This became a problem in pre-school and grade school. In fact, dealing with this problem was a leading motivation in our move to a school in Vancouver, Canada that we felt could best serve her.

It also become a problem with her brother Oliver, who was not fond of being bossed around. Around age 6, we overheard a typical argument outside in the yard. **Leah** told her

brother, "You need to understand that your life will be much better if you just do exactly what I say."

Helping Leah identify and understand her primary fear—an unpredictable world where there is no one to care for her—was vital in helping her come to terms with her bossy behavior. Initially it required a completely different form of parenting. For children like Oliver who have never had a doubt about their safety or how much they are loved, the parenting process involves a slow, measured opening up of the world before them. For children like Leah, it involves closing it down and creating a safe space with firm boundaries so that they don't have to fear for their safety. Our therapist likened it to a child sitting on a stool in a pitch-black room. If they can reach out and feel the walls around them, they can feel safe.

At age 8, we started helping Leah identify this fear through The 5000 Days Project. She loved her sessions with Daddy and was actually fearless in trying to understand herself. The more she came to realize that her bossiness came from a fear of not controlling her world, the more she was able to become its master. Years later, she is no longer bossy with friends… but she still does not hesitate telling her brother what to do.

■

ANOTHER EXAMPLE INVOLVES KIDS who are

procrastinators. Leaving things until the last moment makes their lives hell and the same for their families. When asked if their lives would be better if they did not procrastinate, they universally say, "Yes."

However, when asked why they procrastinate, they often blame it on laziness. When asked to describe their schedules, a familiar answer is, "I wake up at 5:45 and go for a run. I'm out of the shower by 6:25, get dressed, eat breakfast, and get on the bus by 7:18. I go to my study group before classes begin and then..." After school and into the late evening goes the same way. You get the picture. "You're just lazy" is a false narrative that they have bought into for lack of a better explanation. No wonder they cannot solve their procrastination problem when they are addressing it as laziness. What's the answer? To make their life even *busier*. No.

The *real* answer? To get that, you need to identify the chief fear. Most procrastinators are perfectionists and, for a perfectionist, the chief fear is *being imperfect*. So, if a perfectionist leaves work until the last moment and does not earn a perfect score, the failure can be blamed on leaving the work until the last moment. By contrast, if a perfectionist completes work ahead of time and *still* fails to get a perfect score... well, that's imperfection, a *real* failure!

Walking through this realization of fears with a perfectionist is one of the great pleasures of doing what I do. In many cases perfectionists are brilliant, high-level achievers. Realizing that their less-than-perfect tendency to procrastinate is actually a product of their own fears and hence within their grasp to address is a thrilling revelation for them. Obviously, this then opens up the discussion of their source of self-worth (which we discussed in Lesson 6).

■

HERE ARE SOME OF the fears that kids suffer from but cannot identity until the right questions reveal the truth.

♦ Fear of losing their family
♦ Fear of failure
♦ Fear of abandonment or neglect
♦ Fear of rejection
♦ Fear of imperfection
♦ Fear of being unlovable
♦ Fear of being unworthy
♦ Fear of being embarrassed
♦ Fear of too little attention
♦ Fear of too much attention

...and the list goes on. According to Dr. Karl Albrecht writing in *Psychology Today* (March 22, 2012), fear isn't very complicated. It is a feeling, caused by our anticipation of some imagined event or experience which results in a biological reaction based in our amygdala. At times, fear saves our lives because it warns of us danger. Most of the time, however, it plagues us with imaginary worst-case scenarios and gets in the way of being the people we are supposed to be.

Again, *we all live on a continuum between our longings and our fears. Where we are on that spectrum defines how we live our lives*—how optimistic we are, how courageous we are, how many risks we are willing to take and so on. Kids who live closer to their fears are, by nature, more cautious, timid, guarded, and pessimistic. Kids who live closer to their longings are more open, enthusiastic, trusting and optimistic.

Where are *you?*

The Takeaway

What You've Forgotten About Being a Kid:
You think your greatest fear is spiders… and you have no idea how much deeper your fear goes!

What You Can Do About That as an Adult:
Make sure you are aware of your own fears. If you are not, they are likely controlling you. And help your children identify and articulate their fears. Once those fears are exposed and articulated, they will start to lose power.

The Puppet Factor

21 Things You Forgot About Being a Kid

Whether you know it or not, you are *some*thing's little puppet!

YOU KNOW—THAT SPINELESS little toy without a mind of its own?

One of the most talented kids to come through the Prodigy Camp had half a million followers on Social Media. He had a gift for making people laugh while also being extremely dark and edgy.

During an interview, he told me about the dark side of his year. He had gotten in with the wrong bunch of friends, had experimented with almost every kind of drug, and had even tried to "take too many pills." As we started to dig into what was going on, it became clear that he was angry. Extremely so. The source was connected to something that had been happening with his youngest brother... and the resultant anger led him to make a series of self-destructive decisions. This was a big clue because he was way too smart to be making these decisions in his normal, rational state. Everything suddenly made sense.

I normally just ask questions, but in this case I asked if he wanted answers. He did. I replied, "Your problem is that you're anger's little puppet."

He looked at me indignantly. "Hey, I ain't no one's little puppet."

"Okay," I replied. "You're anger's *big* puppet then." He looked at me half confused and half amused.

"Think about it," I said. "Whether consciously or not, you have been trying to hurt yourself with various degrees of effectiveness for over a year now... ever since the 'event' happened. Why would you possibly do that to yourself? You wouldn't, unless something else had control over you. And sure enough, whenever you felt the anger rise in you, you'd go do something stupid. You're lucky you're alive."

He stared at me then dropped his head, shaking it slowly. "Oh, my God. I'm anger's little puppet." A grin of irony crept across his face.

Now, in the interest of full disclosure, given the boy's Rap/Gangsta roots I actually used the "B-word" in this exchange because it spoke to him—but I don't wish to give currency to that word given all it represents. Yet within the space of that hour, he was able to identify the problem and de-personalize it. He was able see that he was not inherently bad but that he had simply allowed something to influence his behavior in such a dangerous way that it had almost destroyed him.

At the same time, the first twelve years of my *own*

122

life made perfect sense. The anger, the consequences—all culminating in that ridiculous march down the middle of my street from my garage-band practice! I had also been anger's puppet until I decided not to be.

Later I would suffer from impatience. My frustration would tend to result in some impulsive action, some insensitive comment, some hastily-written e-mail that should not have been sent. And accordingly, I would reap the consequences of my impatience. Impatience was my master and I was its puppet.

This problem would persist well into my adult years. In fact, my kids would say it still rears its ugly head in me at stop lights and when following day-dreaming drivers. Whenever I start calling someone "sport," my kids know that the battle is going on within me. However, in most areas of my life, I have solved this problem through The 5000 Days Project. What better way to deal with impatience than to start a project that never ends? Yes, I will never reach the end of this project while I'm alive. There; I found a way to make impatience *my* puppet.

I have come to realize that each and every one of us is something's puppet. We all know the alien that takes control of our friends or loved ones when drugs, alcohol, sex, or gambling come into the picture. To paraphrase Ben Franklin writing in *Poor Richard's Almanac* (1739), a man often believes he's become the master of something when he's really becoming a slave to it.

Of course, today, the most common addiction among kids is video games and technology. Most of our kids (and most of us) have become our devices' puppet. And if that word stings every time I use it, it's meant to sting. Remember when "they" said the advent of computers would lead to more leisure time? Four-day weekends? What happened to that? Who's fooling whom? Who's working for whom?

Seeing the robotic obsession kids have with their phones would be funny if it were not so troubling. What happened to hanging out and talking? Most parties consist of kids huddled over their phones. At 15 years old, my two youngest kids ended up being the oldest kids in their school without phones thanks to our family rules. They were good sports about it, especially when 9- and 10-year-olds walked by flaunting their smart phones. My daughter, who just turned 16, has just recently gotten her first phone but despite the time limits we put on it, she still has the glare of a crack monkey when using it. Sorry, Leah, we're going to keep pulling you back from the abyss!

But even if we don't have an addiction, other forces that enslave us include: anger, greed, achievement, envy, adrenaline, impatience, jealousy, popularity, failure, perfection, fashion, resentment, peer pressure, hatred, revenge, desperation, vanity, control… and the list goes on ad infinitum. I have endless stories of kids who are driven by an absolute need to win and while society rewards them, they become a slave to it—chasing a moving goal line. It will never bring them what they really need.

We all know stories about kids who, in their quest for popularity, lose the best part of themselves. And we all know the stories of their wannabee-sidekick-hangers-on who follow their leaders like children afraid of getting lost or left behind.

We all know stories of people who have allowed themselves to become perfection's puppet. The result? Paralysis.

We all know stories of people obsessed with their appearance. As they age, they just become more desperate.

We all know people who are stressed by the thought of losing. Perfect example: **Sam** was one of the fastest kids in his class. Whenever he went to Cross Country meets, everyone expected him to win. That pressure eventually led him to feel sick and nauseous before every meet. What if he lost? Would everyone feel let down? What else would his identify be? He liked being thought of as fast and a winner. But the pressure was making him sick.

I asked him what identity he had beyond being fast and a winner. He said that he thought people viewed him as kind and caring, a good friend, a smart student. (He was actually being modest. Sam is hugely liked and admired at his school.) I asked him: If he lost, would his parents disown him? He shook his head. Would his friends stop liking him? He shrugged, then shook his head. Would the world end? He smiled then started to realize the ridiculous amount of pressure he was putting himself under.

I told Sam to close his eyes and imagine wearing a backpack. I told him to take the many fears plaguing him—fear of losing stature, fear of disappointing others, fear of disappointing himself—and place them in that backpack. I asked him to how it felt. He replied, "Heavy." I then asked him, "Are you going to run your race faster carrying that heavy backpack or are you going to run that race faster without it?"

"Without it," he replied. I told him that once he put his fear in perspective, once he learned that losing his fear was more important than losing any race, once he had the emotional intelligence to drop the fricken backpack, he could run his best and whatever followed, winning or losing, would be okay. It would not change who he was. Besides, if he was not losing some of the time, he was not challenging himself enough.

Now, in the interest of fullest disclosure, my own current master is the future. I am the future's puppet. I love planning, dreaming, and working toward the future—often at the cost of living in the present. Over the last five years I've been working on this and discovering that, as they say, the past is history, the future is fantasy; all we have is the everlasting present, so why not live there? As I try to soak up each moment of daily life with my wife and kids, I realize that time is our rarest commodity and that the only way to stretch it is to live in the present.

Identifying our master is the first step in freeing ourselves and gaining our freedom.

The Takeaway

What You've Forgotten About Being a Kid:
You may think you are in control... but even if you don't, the reality is this: you are *some*thing's puppet!

What You Can Do About That as an Adult:
Discover what or who your own master is, then ask yourself if you are happy being its (their) puppet. Realize the opportunity before you. Recognizing your own fear is the first step to earning your "get out of jail free" card. Free yourself... and then help your children do the same.

Lesson 13

Misunderstood

21 Things You Forgot About Being a Kid

You believe nobody "gets" you.

ALMOST A DECADE AGO, I held auditions in
Australia for The 5000 Days Project. An 11-year-old girl
came in who was quirky and thoughtful. She seemed
beyond her years and anxious to be a part of the project.
At one point in the interview, however, she just started
crying. Now, this is not uncommon as kids dare to
unpeel layers of the onion called their feelings. A girl in
Canada once described the process as "a cleanse for your
mind, a chance expel the toxins, leaving you feeling clear-
headed, refreshed, and renewed." If a kid *does* experience
such feelings, the grand majority of the time the process
ends up as "a cleanse for your mind." But this was not
the case here. This Australian girl kept crying and
crying—and she *left* crying despite my attempts to bring
her back with questions about gratitude or her longings.

I immediately contacted her mother to tell her
about this reaction and expressed my concern. I wanted
to see if she had professional support. Her mother
confirmed that she did and that she often had this

reaction when discussing her feelings. Knowing that the girl had a difficult relationship with her father who was not directly in her life, I also was worried about the possible existence of something much darker underlying her tears. Her mother said that she knew of nothing that might confirm that concern. I asked her to pass on my thoughts to her daughter's psychologist and her mother said the psychologist was equally at a loss. Despite all of this, to my surprise, the girl expressed a keen desire to be selected for the project. Given her desire and, thinking that the process might help her work out whatever was underlying her feelings, I agreed.

At age 12, the girl came in again and the same thing happened. As we started exploring her feelings, the only thing that became clear was that she felt misunderstood, that no one in the world "got her." I again checked in with her mother and we had the same discussion with the same result.

At age 13, it all happened again. *Ground Hog Day.* She expressed sadness over the fact that no one understood her and then she left, crying.

The next year her mother said she had decided against continuing the project. I was fine with that since this was one of those rare cases where the StoryQ process did not seem to be working. Every once in a while, a child will discover something about themselves that makes them feel so uncomfortable or so exposed that continuing is frightening to them. In those cases, my response is always the same. I honor their decision, I do my best to make sure they have the right parental and/or professional help, and finally I let them know they are welcome to come back at any time.

About half of the time, those kids come back. Such was the case recently with a 12-year-old Canadian boy who had been equally confused about the forces working within him. His mother wrote and shared that the interview had made him sad—that it had opened up some big feelings he had had about his father not spending enough time with him and that it had all spilled out in a tearful epiphany a month later. She said that father and son had since made a huge effort to carve out more time together and that as a result things were much better. However, she said that she did not want her son to feel sad again.

I pulled up my notes and found that the biggest fear in this boy's family was anyone having to experience sadness. It reminded me of my own family where harmony was more highly valued than truth and how that had led to important things not being said. I replied to this mother in my usual way but also shared that emotions are valuable clues to truth and that the sadness had been the catalyst of healing. I pointed out that a rich life is not just a happy life; it is a life that encompasses the entire range of emotions and that sadness was nothing to be scared of. To her credit, she made the connection and sure enough, her son came back for his

13-year-old interview, a new boy, anxious to do the work to know himself better.

In the Australian girl's case the same thing happened. After skipping a year she wanted to come back and continue. However, unlike the Canadian boy, she had no such epiphany. In fact, at 15, she came in and cried harder than ever. As I attempted to get to the bottom of these emotions, it always came down to feeling misunderstood.

Over the next couple years she got into drugs, an abusive relationship, and some self-destructive behavior. Still, she kept coming back for more.

For a while I had had a suspicion. This girl's issue was not being misunderstood by others. That was a projection. Her real issue what that she misunderstood herself and the more she blamed it on others, the more she managed to avoid exploring the very thing that could heal her. *That* was the greatest harm she was doing herself. During the next interview, I pointed this out and to her credit she took it in. In the last few years, in interview after interview, she has discovered in herself this amazing person that may well go out and change the world. She is full of caring, generosity, and a passion to protect nature and its creatures.

If I have any wish for the kids in my project, it is that they realize the power of their own agency. My wish is that they become the main character in their own story and not a secondary character in someone else's story.

Recalling this Australian girl's history has made me realize that all of us feel misunderstood at times—as kids *and* as adults. And despite our efforts on Facebook to project our perfect selves, as it has been often said, "all any of us really want is to be known for who we are and be loved anyway."

However, before any of that can occur, we need to know ourselves. Otherwise, how can we expect anyone else to truly know us?

So when you hear yourself saying "No one understands me," the subtext is likely to be, "I don't understand me." The good news is that once you discover who truly holds the key to "knowing you," that person (you!) can start to solve the problem.

The Takeaway

What You've Forgotten About Being a Kid:
You often—maybe even *always*—feel that no one understands you.

What You Can Do About That as an Adult:
Stealing an idea from Parker Palmer, the 5000 Days Project team early on adopted one mission description as "Helping Kids Find Themselves Before They Lose Themselves." Growing up is tough, and it's often very difficult sorting out who we really are from who others (and

ourselves!) *expect* us to be. The net result is that we often don't *begin* to know who we really are... which makes it impossible for *others* to know us! Instead of fussing so much over your kids' grades, help them first get to know themselves. After all, Socrates didn't say "Know math." He said, "Know thyself." Everything else will follow.

Sucks

21 Things You Forgot About Being a Kid

.

Fourteen sucks.

ON PRETTY MUCH EVERY LEVEL.

Obviously, that's not 100% true. Sometimes ages 13 and 15 suck too. While a select few kids have skated unscathed through this difficult period, the grand majority go through some form of "gauntlet of adolescence." This is the period where decisions are made and actions are taken that can affect the rest of their lives. Kids shift into survival mode and the values of childhood are tested. They reside in a constant state of vigilance, unsure about their social, emotional or even physical safety. As with runners of all gauntlets, some make it through unscathed, while some make it through with some scar tissue… and some don't make it at all.

■

NICKI WAS AN ENGAGING, attractive tomboy who excelled at everything, especially sports. When I started interviewing her at age 10 she could hold her own with

any of the boys. In fact, they were all quite taken by her— a dream girl to fellow 10-year-old boys. Her goal was to become a sports broadcaster.

When **Nicki** made transition into young womanhood, however, she became increasingly bothered by her perceived imperfections. Some days she was fine going to school in sweats and looking like she had just worked out. Other days, she was paralyzed by the thought of not looking perfect.

At age 14, she figured the solution was to lose some weight. Within months, she was hospitalized, days away from losing her life to an eating disorder.

SIMON WAS ATHLETIC, SMART, handsome and popular. Everybody wanted to be Simon. He won awards including student of the month at his middle school and was nearly unbeatable at wrestling. He came from a stellar family until that stellar family imploded. As the most sensitive member of his family, his world fell apart. Now age 14, he sought pain relief in drugs, eventually developing a heroin habit—something from which few individuals ever recover. One day he just disappeared.

A week went by. Then two. Then a month. No one knew where he was. Due to dumb luck, I passed him waiting for somebody on the side of a road. I turned my car around and went back to talk with him. He told me that he was waiting for his girlfriend. She was getting a car and they were driving to California. I told him that everyone was missing him. He shrugged but I could tell he was conflicted. I asked him if he wanted me to give him a ride home. He shook his head. We talked a bit longer. I asked him what he wanted. That question stumped him. I told him that I was going to wait there with him until his girlfriend came and, if at any time he wanted me to bring him home, that I would do. After a long moment he asked me to bring him home.

■

SREY PEL'S PARENTS DIED before her 5th birthday leaving her and her siblings with their aunt, and eventually the Sunrise

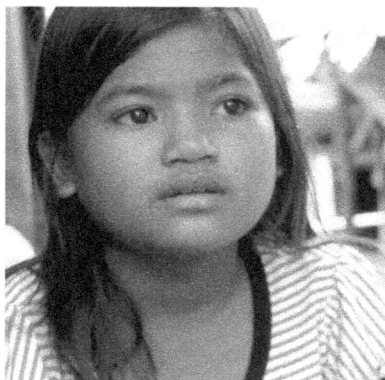

Orphanage. Srey Pel thrived at Sunrise both academically and athletically. In fact, she could beat any boy at any sport and was the model of a strong girl. Taking advantage of Sunrise's groundbreaking kickboxing program, she became nationally competitive with plans to earn money to help her older brother, who was having financial challenges with his new business. She also wanted to use her education to become a doctor and save people like her parents.

Around age 14, however, she realized she liked other girls—a difficult revelation in a country that has not yet accepted that women, like men, might be homosexual. Her older brothers and sisters felt this was a disgrace to the family and said they would reject her if she did not change back to liking boys. They also said that becoming a "girl kickboxer" would bring further disgrace to the family and that she should not compete. On top of all that, the girl she had fallen in love with betrayed her and broke her heart.

At that point, she stopped listening to her inner voice and started listening to her older brothers and sisters… because when you don't have parents, your remaining family is everything. She was stuck between two competing fears: first, the fear of losing the only family she had left; and second, the fear of not being who she is.

One night several months ago, she tried taking too many pills and ended up in the hospital at 2 a.m. getting her stomach pumped. Upon her recovery, Sunrise mum Geraldine assured her how much she loved her, but Srey Pel's pain was not assuaged. She replied: "But you love everyone. I want someone who loves only me."

She then admitted that, at night, she hears her mother speaking to her from beyond the grave. She hears two things. She wants Srey Pel to be who she is, but Srey Pel also thinks she wants her to come join her.

■

DIEGO DID HIS FIRST interview at age 10 when we established the project in San Miguel de Allende in Mexico. He came from a caring middle class family, could run circles around most people with a soccer ball, and captured the eyes of girls and probably some boys with his dark good looks. He was one of the few kids, along with his older brother, Jose Maria, capable of doing the interview in English. His father was an artist and engineer who, along with his mother, highly valued education and travel.

By the time his 14-year-old interview came around, our families had become great friends, and during a dinner together I learned of a deeply disturbing event that had happened to them. Diego's father shared with me that the local mafia had extorted the family's life saving under threat of leaving Diego and Jose Maria's severed heads on their porch. He made one payment only to have the mafia demand more. Now they had no money and this common crime targeting middle class families did not merit the attention of the police.

Diego's father did not know what to do and was deeply stressed—to the point of being sick. We discussed various plans including their entire family moving to Spain. We then had to leave to go back home, so we kept in touch via e-mail.

Sadly, within the next couple months, the stress got to be too much. Diego's father fell ill and died just a few weeks later. Diego's mother was one of the best mothers in the world, but she had to go right to work just to keep up with house payments and to keep the family fed. Suddenly, both Diego and Jose Maria found themselves grief-stricken, fatherless, and penniless.

Jose Maria, who had suffered a traumatic back injury from parkour several months before, increased his dose of medical marijuana just to deal with the pain. Diego did all he could, working for a dollar per hour in a local restaurant and trying to keep up with school; but eventually he fell into a deep sadness. It was a sadness that ran so deep that his older brother's drugs seemed to be the only means of relieving his pain...

■

AT AGE 14, I did not have to struggle with an eating disorder, or my family falling apart, or doubts about my sexuality, or the pain of losing a parent. On the surface, I was extremely lucky; but even I remember doubting the purpose of my existence and experiencing a tsunami of emotions that included hopelessness and resignation.

This is where a number of we adults got stuck in some form of arrested development, thanks to some trauma that we now barely remember. All we know is that, for strange and unpredictable reasons, certain situations make us palpably sad or anxious. For instance, we might be terrified to speak in front of groups due to fear of embarrassment; or we have trouble trusting people because of a sense of impending betrayal. The list of symptoms goes on and on, sometimes with less drama, sometimes with more.

As the stories above demonstrate, trials *can* create amazing human beings. A lucky few are like the phoenix, being reborn, rising from the ashes. The gauntlet of adolescence might even be compared to "rites of passage" that primitive cultures used to practice to develop their young men and woman. The main difference, however, is that those rituals were carefully designed and guided to take the child through the challenge safely. Beyond the general objective of keeping our kids out of harm's way, we have no such safety net as our kids negotiate the dangers of a world that changes at breathtaking speed. Since the turn of the 21st Century, the full power of the Internet, with its unlimited ability to access everything, has been put in the hands of most children in the both developed world and developing world.

This leads us again to the proposition we touched on at the end of Lesson 13: **Is it possible, during adolescence, for kids to find themselves before they lose themselves?**

The good news is that, based on my 5500+ interviews, there seems to be a sweet spot between ages 9-12 where kids *can* be armed and equipped to face this gauntlet. When kids are asked the right questions, develop their values, and identify their priorities, they are less likely to make dangerous decisions during this period. Of course there is no substitute for a close family where parents and other mentors are involved. But sometimes even those kids from the best of families take a wrong turn unless they have prepared themselves for the outside world.

For instance, a kid who is interested in being a doctor is less likely to get high before going to school every day at age fourteen, intuiting that that activity won't get them where they want to go. Again, how are kids supposed to get to where they want to go if they don't know how to articulate the destination?

The Takeaway

What You've Forgotten About Being a Kid:
Early adolescence sucks.

What You Can Do About That as an Adult:
Knowing that "the gauntlet" is coming, we can start talking to our kids about it as they approach their teens… and, knowing it will come, we can structure our own lives to be *more* available as it creeps up rather than *less*. Don't get burned out on parenting before you hit the big leagues. If the teen years was where *you* were abandoned by your well-meaning but bewildered parents, don't repeat the mistake. Stick with it. Slow and steady wins the race.

Mortality, and the Beautiful Side of Sorrow

21 Things You Forgot About Being a Kid

You believe death can't touch you. Until it does.

MY GRANDPARENTS USED TO live in Bellevue, Washington which is across Lake Washington from Seattle. Before the first floating bridge was built, we had to drive all the way around the lake to visit them. On one occasion, my once-vibrant and loving grandmother had spent our entire visit looking pale, sleeping on the couch, barely conscious. I had never seen her like this before. I was deeply disturbed and asked my parents about her. On the long return trip, in the darkness of the backseat of our green Dodge, I first learned about death. The fact that we were all eventually going to die.

I don't remember obsessing over it. I don't remember being afraid of it. I just remember the feeling of emptiness that the news inspired. I was 6 years old.

I also don't remember thinking much about death *after* that.

Teenage feelings of immortality are well documented, and certainly my 5500+ interviews have done nothing to change the point of view. I do remember returning from Christmas break during my sophomore year of high school to find the desk ahead of mine in my math class empty. Mel Stone had been killed in a sledding accident. We were all stunned that one of our own could be taken before his time.

I have seen this reality hit kid after kid—either through losing a friend to suicide (now the second-leading cause of death among kids), a car accident, or sickness. For every generation, there are the "sacrificial lambs" who remind us that we are, indeed, mortal beings.

Making sense of an untimely death, however, seems beyond our abilities. And so we bury it. Our minds don't do well with things of which we can't make sense. Sure, we can look for causes—there *are* the physical realities. We need air, we need sustenance, we need shelter from the elements to survive. The human body, when met with cement, steel, or lead at a certain velocity, does not fare well. But none of these *facts* really add up to a result so emotionally permanent as confronting death.

A friend of mine, Dr. Jennifer Stuber, founded the suicide prevention center at the University of Washington after her husband shot himself. He left behind two young children, both of whom are in The 5000 Days Project. The oldest, Jake, was 6 years old when he lost his father, and during the memorial service—when everyone was reflecting on this

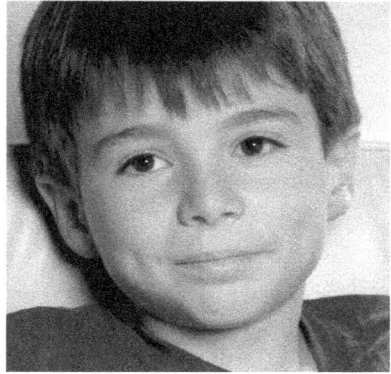

accomplished man's life— **Jake** put his finger to his head and pulled an imaginary trigger to demonstrate how it happened. The gathering was shocked, but Jake was right. Everyone could speculate, *and* celebrate after a fashion… but what killed Jake's father was a bullet from a gun. Accordingly, a lot of Jenn's work has focused on the practical issues we can identify and comprehend—the improper storage of guns, the visible signs of hopelessness, the quest for some form of pain relief. Jenn's work does not try to make sense of it all, because often there simply is no making sense of it.

When you add untimely, senseless deaths to the endless barrage of violent news and images kids are exposed to every day, we shouldn't be surprised that kids have difficulty processing all of it. But as I personally discovered, simply putting off the processing does not make it go away. The emotion still resides somewhere inside of you, eating at you from the inside.

So how do kids express their feelings about death? How do they attempt to make sense of end-of-life issues?

The first time death really came home for me was when my grandfather passed away. I was 11 years old, and that was the first time I saw my father cry. This was one of the first times I remember feeling deep, almost unmanageable sorrow.

The topic of death does not come up more than any other in my interviews, but the evidence of sorrow is almost always present. It normally arises around the death or sickness of a grandparent or a favorite pet. In fact, the latter often produces the *most* outpouring of sadness. This may be because the death of a pet represents a first-hand loss; but I also think the death of a pet—or, to a similar extent, a grandparent—represents a safe, acceptable catch-all for all of the sorrow in a child's life.

I was recently interviewing a 16-year-old who was completely stoic when talking about his parents' recent divorce. The breakup had come somewhat out of the blue, and I knew that family had been the greatest priority in this young man's life—the thing for which he always felt most grateful. Yet he either could not or would not express his feelings about the divorce. I asked if he'd spoken to his brother and sister about it, and he had not. Even though they were all suffering a similar tragedy in the closest of proximity, they did not have the vocabulary to express their "sad," and comfort one another.

About the same time, however, his dog has been diagnosed with cancer and they had to put him down. He was very clear about his emotions surrounding this sad coincidence. I do believe that pets represent innocence, and hence the sadness surrounding losing them is uncomplicated. However, I also think that they become a conduit for everything sad and sorrowful in their lives.

Because sadness is perceived as a negative emotion—one that involves feelings we'd rather not feel, feelings that supposedly make us weak and vulnerable—my work with kids has made it plain that we don't do a good job of teaching kids the role of sorrow in our lives. Hence, they are either devastated by it or try to deny it. Either way, they are not processing it; and as long as they don't, it too will eat them like a cancer. Physically *and* emotionally.

To help kids process these feelings, I start by asking them something that seems obvious: Why are they sad? People and animals die every day. What is different here? Whether it is the death of a pet or a grandparent, the answer always gets down to "Because I loved them." While I'm not in the habit of quoting Winnie the Pooh, A.A. Milne's words always help introduce the beautiful side of sadness. To paraphrase, when Pooh loses someone he says, "Aren't I so lucky to have loved someone so much that it hurts so much when they're gone?"

Death hurts because we're losing something special to us, something not everyone will have the privilege of experiencing. Feeling sadness is a way of honoring what we've lost.

Does that mean that pain is a by-product of loving something or someone? That there can be no joy without sorrow? What a powerful thing to watch children mature before my very eyes as they contemplate this. You can see the wheels turning, minds processing feelings they have been trying to deny or ignore. Whether the source of sorrow be a death or even a painful breakup, I ask them the ultimate question: "If you had a chance to *never* feel this pain again but also never feel the love that *preceded* it... or love *again* knowing that pain and sorrow is a part of it, what would you choose?"

Nine out of ten kids choose the latter.

The Takeaway

What You've Forgotten About Being a Kid:
You may believe that you'll never die—or you may believe that you'll never grow old. Either way, death really doesn't touch you... until it devastates you.

What You Can Do About That as an Adult:
Let's rediscover and reposition the role of sadness in our lives. Let's not ignore it. Let's not deny it. After all, we cannot do so. It is what it is. Let's embrace sadness as an honest and

healthy emotional celebration of having lost something we dared to love. In acknowledging life's inevitable cycles, we better prepare our kids for their rightful place in it.

Mirror, Mirror, On the Wall

21 Things You Forgot About Being a Kid

You are as good looking as you think you are.

FOR YEARS, I POSED this uncomfortable question: "Take one hundred kids your age. Where among those hundred would you rank yourself in terms of looks, with 100 being the best looking?" In contrast to the other thirty-odd questions—which kids generally enjoyed because they were like solving a puzzle for them—this question was by far their least favorite. They squirmed, saying they didn't know or that they didn't want to seem conceited. I told them not to worry about sounding conceited; this was just a simple question about how they perceived themselves. They reluctantly got around to a number.

By the end of interviews, though, something extraordinary happened. They would *become the number they gave*. This in spite of what number society *might* have given them at first glance. Of course, this "you are what you feel you are" phenomenon is not particularly ground-breaking, psychologically; but seeing the evolution of the process unfold before me was fascinating. A stunningly beautiful girl with low self-esteem might say, "I'm around 20," and mean it without a shred of false humility. On the flipside, an average looking boy might say, "99!" and grin as wide as the Grand Canyon. And sure enough, their level of self-confidence and self-esteem and degree of egocentricity would bear out the uttered number by the end of the interview. The average looking boy would become more attractive, and the beautiful girl would become less so.

Obviously, beauty is subjective; but there are certain features that society seems to agree upon and cause some people to end up with modeling contracts or getting cast in movies. Thanks to the billions of dollars that advertisers spend each year to let us know how badly we each need their products, shared ideas of what is beautiful are thrown at us in media from the moment we can sit up and watch television. Hence, the question I have asked, as awkward as it is, is helpful in identifying how much children's self-images have been influenced by such external influences. This is especially true as it relates to body image.

In my analysis, two things stood out as interesting. First, girls generally rated themselves lower than boys... although only *after* they entered their teen years. Up to age 11, girls and boys were somewhat even in the degree of attention they paid to their looks. That changed with puberty, however. Despite decades of feminism, the messages that a girl's self-worth is tied directly to her level of attractiveness to boys/men are still alive and well—though more subtly played.

Sometimes, it even occurs earlier. One of my original kids was **Jade**, a blond-haired, blue-eyed beauty who at age 9 came in with glitter on her face and wanting to be Britney Spears. Despite being one of the sweetest people I've ever met, even at this young age she was obsessed with having a boyfriend and felt quite competitive with her fellow fourth-grade girls.

When Jade became a teenager, things took a serious turn for the worse. She got extremely depressed, feeling constantly judged by those around her—including her father who, according to her, would comment on her weight. By age 15, she was diagnosed with body dysmorphic disorder. BDD is a psychiatric anomaly where the individual is obsessed with personal appearance and sees a monster in the mirror.

Jade ended up dropping out of school, developing a drug habit, and getting arrested. During this period she would miss our scheduled interviews, in part, because they required asking hard questions of herself. While recovering in treatment, she discovered she was pregnant. And then something amazing happened. Her maternal instincts kicked in. Losing all interest in her own looks, she decided to keep the baby and clean up her life. She finished treatment and went cold turkey. **Jade** repaired her relationships, paid off her fines and determined that nothing would ever be more important than that which was best for her little girl. Against all odds and with the help of her family, she had the child, went back to school and has recently gotten married. She has become one of the best mothers in the world and that sweet side that was so apparent in her youth now radiates again as she becomes the woman she was always meant to be.

On the flip side, there are some girls who push through puberty without ever become obsessed with their looks. Based on my interviews, I would say that the biggest influence involves a strong female role-model, most likely a mother. Equally as important is a father who helps build self-esteem based on core values and character traits versus appearance. Other contributing factors can include finding other passions and goals like sports, service, or academics—anything that does not leave a lot of time to obsess about boys. While there are positives and negatives to single-sex schools, there is an argument for allowing girls to find their extraordinary selves *before* having to deal with boys.

For boys, the biggest issue is body image involving weight, build, or height. They are either too heavy, too skinny, not tall enough, or they need more muscles. In general, however, the self-esteem of boys seems less tied to their looks.

What is more interesting is the extent to which beauty can be a plague. That seems like a ridiculous statement on the surface. Most of us ask, "If beauty is a plague, then where can I catch it?" But as the saying goes, "Be careful what you wish for."

Life *does* come easier for beautiful people, at a certain level. More people want to be their friends, they get chosen for leadership positions more frequently, they have an easier time attracting romantic interests. But we often gravitate toward where we get our strokes. If a good looking person is constantly getting affirmation for being good-looking, and then buys into that affirmation and bases self-worth on appearance, it can become a curse. They don't *have* to work has hard, so they don't *learn* to work as hard; and when their beauty fades—which it will—all they are left with is a weak work ethic.

I started interviewing **one such boy** when he was 12. He already had achieved a lot of attention for his looks and he came to rely upon them. Not many years passed, however, before **he** started feeling isolated and lonely. He grew suspicious of why people liked him and started withdrawing. Thanks to a good family, he reined himself back in to what counts—but the process was not without some confusion and unhappiness.

The Takeaway

What You've Forgotten About Being a Kid:
You are just as attractive as you think you are.

What You Can Do About That as an Adult:
By the time we have become adults, we have all been through our own obsessions and insecurities with our looks. None of us has escaped the multi-billion dollar industry dedicated to convincing us that our self-worth should be based on our appearance. Add that to the forces of nature during puberty and we have the perfect storm creating an unhealthy relationship with our physical appearance.

Despite and perhaps because of the above, it is all the more important to be extremely cognizant of the messages we send to our kids about the importance of looks. As with "fake news," the only way to combat this untruth is by acknowledging the insidious way it functions in our lives and calling it for what it is. This is not to say we should be unconcerned with the way we look. We just need to put that concern in its proper place.

Prejudice, and Pride

21 Things You Forgot About Being a Kid

Your parents sure are a lot more hung up on racial differences and sexual preferences than you are.

IF AN AMERICAN MIDDLE school could have a mayor, he would have been it. Despite being only 12 years old, scrawny, and speaking broken English, Cristian lit up the school with his electric smile and confident personality. He had only recently arrived from Mexico with his mother and older siblings, and the plan was for their father to come join them. They lived in a small, modest apartment but felt at least as rich as everyone else because they had each other and were grateful to be in America. Cristian boasted traditional values, and when asked about girls, he warned about some of them wanting to get too close and that he was "not that type of people."

Two years later of course, he started getting very interested in girls and ended up dating another immigrant. She was from Korea. He fell head over heels in love with her only to have her father, who didn't want her dating a Mexican, attempt to take out a restraining order on him after an incident at school. The father did not know Cristian. He did not know about his beautiful spirit or rock-solid family values. All he knew was that he was a Mexican immigrant.

I stood in court with Cristian as he tried to describe to the female judge in his broken English what had happened. The judge sided with the girl's family and he was ordered to stay away. He was crushed. This was the first of a few setbacks for Cristian, including his father failing to join the family from Mexico… and the discovery when he was 19 that he was in America illegally! He immediately came forward and signed up for the Obama administration's DACA program… only to have President Trump put it on hold and start deporting those who had honorably come forward. The immigration debate is a valid one; but this country is richer because of a person like Cristian.

■

GWENTH'S PARENTS WERE FROM Vietnam. She studied hard in school and sought to integrate while following her parent's rules—that is, until those two opposing priorities collided. After returning from an event with friends where American boys had been present, her father attacked her with a whipping branch from a tree. After breaking the branch on her, he went outside to find a new one and she barricaded herself in her room until the next day when he went to work. She left home and reported the incident to social services.

■

THESE ARE FAMILIAR IMMIGRANT stories where generational conflicts are amplified by cultural conflicts. "Agonizing" is a good word to describe watching immigrant kids struggle with the all-consuming issues of growing up and being accepted while also trying to honor their parents' traditions and values. Likewise, their parents' frightened and confused attempts to raise them in a second language in a foreign land are equally agonizing to witness. However, these immigrant stories are simply a manifestation of a generational conflict that is pervasive and as old as time: Protective parents try to safeguard their offspring against unpredictable forces of change, while kids who face change *constantly* are prepared for it… and are less invested in the status quo. As a result, kids are more open to sexual and racial diversity than their parents. Always. After all, intolerance and racism are learned—a product of fearful-love "nurture," not nature.

Throughout the years, I have often thrown out social questions in my interviews to see where kids were on various issues. Do they support gay marriage? Are they "Right to Life" or "Pro-Choice"? How do they feel about a person's "right to die," or the death penalty? What is their position on gun control?

Could they ever takes someone's life or give up their own and, if so, under what circumstances?

Depending on their age, kids either mirror their parents' opinions on these various issues or they are on the more tolerant side of them. I do not remember one case where their position was less tolerant.

Of all these issues, the most dynamic by far has been that involving sexual preference and gay marriage. At the turn of the millennium, most Americans opposed gay marriage. When elected in 2008, even Barack Obama was on record as opposing it. It was Joe Biden, his Vice President, who, in a classic Biden gaffe, inadvertently forced President Obama to reconsider his position.

Much has been said about the 80/20 generational phenomenon. 80% of 80-year-olds opposed gay marriage while 20% supported it. Alternatively, 20% of 20-year-olds opposed gay marriage while 80% supported it. And so the numbers reflected a similar position based on age. 40% of 40-year-olds opposed it, 50% of 50-year-olds, and so on. And sure enough, 10% of 10-year-olds opposed it while 90% believed a person should be allowed to marry whomever they wanted to marry.

■

AS PREVIOUSLY MENTIONED, JONATHAN was one of the original kids who joined The 5000 Days Project in 2001. He was a typical white teenager dealing with the typical issues of being accepted. He ran and won for student council and asked one of the prettiest girls in school to the prom. A year later, however, he had been arrested for shoplifting and was having violent outbreaks in his otherwise peaceful home. He was also sneaking out a night and having sex with men. Fourteen of them in six months to be exact. He hated this side of himself and did all he could to deny it. That denial, pain and conflict led to a drug habit and more domestic turmoil. His caring parents did not know what to do. After things blew up, he eventually came to terms with who he really was and, once he accepted himself, his life came together. He has since become a highly successful adult and an articulate advocate for gay rights.

■

CONVERSELY, LIAM CAME OF age ten years later and had an entirely different experience. He went to a progressive school, had loving parents and walked by the mirror one day and said to himself, "Liam, you are so gay." And with that he came out with little angst or fanfare. He went on to McGill University, the Harvard of Canada, and is pursuing graduate studies in environmental sciences.

■

I THINK THE PHENOMENON is directly related to the pace of change, which accelerates every year thanks to the fire-hose of information aimed at our kids. They have somehow figured out a way to drink from it. Whether involving LGBT issues or racial issues, pop culture—primarily via music and sport—has blurred boundaries and developed a new sense of "us." We have our kids to thank for leading the way... just as we once did. Remember?

The Takeaway

What You've Forgotten About Being a Kid: Your parents are *definitely* a lot more hung up on racial differences and sexual preferences than you are.

What You Can Do About That as an Adult: We all marvel at how 4-year-olds playing together do not see race or carry prejudice. My wife, Julie, visited Bodies: The Exhibition and was deeply moved by how we all are truly exactly the same underneath. How do we escape the environmental and social influences that pervert our childlike innocence? We don't. But we *can* be aware of those influences and, in this case, listen and learn from our kids.

Lesson 18:

Ugh

21 Things You Forgot About Being a Kid

You don't... and *do*... want to talk about sex.

I MADE A DELIBERATE decision at the start of the project to not ask questions involving sex. For me, this was the domain of parents and might push personal boundaries too far. Even though I feel pretty relaxed about discussing such things, I have never regretted this decision even though I think it represents a hole in the project. After all, kids need to talk about sex, especially with someone who knows what they are talking about. They certainly get enough "information" from their peers, who are often not coming from a place of knowledge.

All of that said, kids *especially* don't want to talk to adults about it. "I mean, gross, right?" It does not seem to occur to them that they exist because their parents engaged in the very act which they don't wish to contemplate! Gosh, that thought is still even awkward for me, and my parents passed away a decade ago. Maybe when I am older...

Americans, of course, are known to be quite

prudish among Europeans when it comes to things like sex... or even the toilet. For decades, characters on American network television never seemed to have any bowel or bladder needs. I am not sure when this weirdness began, but the words "pee" and "poo" will send shivers of delight and embarrassment through any 4-year-old (or 14- or 34-year-old in arrested development!). Likewise, the mere mention of the word "butt" or "underwear" will cause a similar reaction in any 7-year-old.

From the start, my other least popular question involved asking kids about their crushes. Even the coolest of kids become all awkward about romance. However, one day I was interviewing a 12-year-old boy while fighting a migraine headache. I usually cancel when I am not 100% because I want every kid to get the best from me. In this case, however, canceling was not an option this one specific day so I proceeded a little shy of my usually empathetic approach. In a straight-forward, matter-of-fact way I just asked the question, "Are you in love? Do you have any crushes?" The query was missing the usual tone of "just between you and me." I might have well been asking "Do you brush your teeth before or after meals?" The boy answered in a surprisingly straight-forward way and gave me the full details. It felt good to him to say it out loud.

This was my first of many clues that the exact manner and *attitude* with which I asked a question had a strong projection upon the person I was interviewing. My own slight discomfort with the question had been coloring the responses. Naming crushes is a vital question because, if I am helping them create a video record of their major thoughts and deeds for their own reference in the future, this is something they will want to know. And if they are uncomfortable with the question, they can say so and why—without my own discomfort coloring their response.

A change in my approach reduced the discomfort down from 90% of kids to about 50%. No matter how I ask the question, at least half of the kids are still awkward about it, usually because they either have not admitted a crush to themselves or because they have had a bad result from sharing it with others. Brothers, sisters, and friends can be relentless when entrusted with such confidential information, and it often does not end well.

Every rare once in a while, if I think the kid can take it, I will ask the question: "Where were you when you first learned about how babies are made? Who told you, and was it awkward?" One of the best responses I ever received was from the son of a school principal. He talked about how he was taking a shower at age 12 when his dad came into the bathroom and chose that moment to tell him the facts of life. I know the father well and I can see him thinking, *What a perfect time. I won't have to look at my son while explaining this.* Of course, from the son's point of view, it was Awkward with a capital A.

A lot of parents simply depend upon schools to "have the talk." However, if they don't have "have the talk" themselves, they inadvertently send a message to their kids that sex is a subject not to be discussed. And when those kids need to discuss sexuality for whatever reason, they *will* get their information elsewhere.

Again, the greatest barrier is our own discomfort with it. The solution? Try to check your own awkwardness at the door. After all, the talk will be as awkward as you make it. The more awkward *you* are about it, the more awkward *they* will be about it. Then again, you could make it easy on yourself and just tell them when they're in the shower!

The time that sex and sexuality does enter the conversation is when its consequences have complicated a young person's life, and forced its way in unnaturally.

Several years ago I initiated a longitudinal video study with a group of ninth graders as they made their way through high school. Karla, age 14, had auditioned and had been selected but had not shown up for her interview. About a half an hour into the wait, we received a call from her. She was at the hospital and had thought it was time to have her baby but it turned out being a false alarm. Her *baby*???

The audition had been done on video tape framed from the shoulders up. Sure enough, she came in the next day, eight months pregnant and did her interview. The next four years were an emotional rollercoaster as she tried to navigate being an unwed mother and a high school student. At times she felt suicidal and, at other times, simply exhausted. Thanks to an involved teen father and two strong mothers—but mostly thanks to her pure determination and resilience—she graduated from high school with plans to pursue her doctorate in counseling.

Naturally, kids who find themselves in situations like these cannot avoid talking about sex and its implications.

Sexual and gender identity and preference have also been familiar topics during my interviews as kids discover who they are. Three of them have identified themselves as transgender and many more have identified as gay or lesbian.

One 12-year-old girl was horrified as the reality of her attractions hit her. She sobbed her way through an interview having told no one else. Sure enough, now she is about to graduate and could not be more brilliant, poised, nor confident in herself.

Another boy had a darkness and pessimism about him that was palpable. He expressed this by making extremely dark short films. As he became aware of his preferences he poured all of that raw passion into his work, becoming one of the most promising up-and-coming young directors working today.

Yet another boy was so frightened of his emerging attractions that it took him three years to address it directly in his interview. It was clear from his comments that he wanted and, in fact, *needed* to talk about his sexual orientation. However, he could not bring himself to say the words associated with the subject.

At some stage in every interview, I ask each young person to rate themselves in terms of happiness on a scale of 1-10 with 10 being the happiest. Once they have done this, I ask, "If you could change one thing in your life with a snap of a finger to make that number go up, what would it be?"

The first year this young man answered the question along the lines of "I would be happier if I didn't have to keep this secret I have." I asked him if he wanted to talk about that secret. He said no. I told him that I would be here for him when he did. He nodded cautiously.

The next year I asked him if he was ready to talk about his secret. He shook his head. He then proceeded to tell me how he had felt suicidal that year due to it, though. Again I offered. Again he declined. Realizing that things had gotten potentially dangerous, I assured him of confidentiality and told him I had a pretty good idea what it was. He nodded. I asked him if it would help if I said it. He shook his head. He knew I knew but still did not want it said out loud. Without revealing a thing, I contacted his father and two of his friends and just suggested they keep an eye on him because he was struggling with some things. They all did so.

Finally, the next year, he came in still reluctant to say anything out loud but then proceeded to tell me that he was in love with his best friend—a friend who was straight. We proceeded to talk about the pain of unrequited love. He was creative and we talked about how sometimes creative people feel things deeper than "normal" people. I told him that, whoever we are and whoever we love, we can feel better once we own it and feel pride in it. I asked him if he was certain about his preferences and feelings. He nodded with conviction. I asked him if he could say the words describing his sexual preference out loud. He shook his head. I asked him if he'd like to try and he said no. He did not want to be defined by it.

The rest was obviously up to him. He is quite brilliant on every level and I know that eventually he will work this out and come to own who he is. That said, I fully appreciate his desire to not be defined by any labels.

For this reason, I think sexuality is an area we all can only discover in our own way in our own time. Others can be helpful; but this is something so personal that providing a safe place and a non-judgmental ear is the best anyone else can do.

There are cases when sexual issues are easy to identify before the individual being interviewed even knows... and vice versa. Regarding the latter, I had a chance to do a five-hour 5000 Days Project interview with Troye Sivan at age 16 before he became the pop star he is today. His family invited me to stay with them in Perth for three days while Troye and I discussed everything under the sun—everything he wished to cover, that is. His sexuality was not one of them. I found Troye to be perhaps one of the two or three smartest young people I have ever interviewed and clearly among the most talented. He had the best family in the world—one that actually inspired me when I went back to mine. It would be another 2-3 years before he came out in one of the most honest, profound, and widely-watched videos on YouTube. Clearly he had an idea of his sexuality when I was interviewing him, but he was not ready to discuss it until it was right for him. Having given comfort and confidence to perhaps millions of LGBT kids, I am glad he did what he did and when he did it.

The darkest stories I come across, though, relate to sexual abuse, rape, or incest. Obviously, parents who are abusing their children don't typically allow their kids to

sign up for the project. Sadly, that means that some kids who desperately need help will not get it from this project. However, in many cases of abuse outside the nuclear family, parents simply do not know—as was the case with **Danielle**. Again, these things tend to rise to the surface through previously-unprocessed emotions. Kids eventually have to take themselves back to painful moments in order to start the healing process.

Sadly, the most familiar story relates to girls and date rape. Listening to them process the humiliation and pain, often for the first time, is soul-destroying. The #MeToo movement has been a long time in coming and, while it is essential that we maintain the principle of "innocent until proven guilty," empowering women *and* men who have been victims of sexual abuse can only help reduce such crimes in the future.

Our sexuality is a central part of who we are, and my hunch is that a significant portion of the arrested development adults suffer is related to unprocessed experiences and feelings from this time of discovery. When ready, talking about it provides a road to revelation and healing.

The Takeaway

What You've Forgotten About Being a Kid: You really don't… and *do*… want to talk about sex.

What You Can Do About That as an Adult: Try to identify your own hang-up or unprocessed arrested development surrounding sex so that you can check it at the door before talking to your kids. Then make that connection and make it a healthy one for them. If you don't, someone else will.

Lesson 19

The Anatomy of Cool

It has never occurred to you that, at one point in their lives, your parents might actually have been cool.

LET'S FACE IT: WE all look like fashion or trend victims in our old pictures. Your kids have seen the photos on the wall when you were young, handsome, or beautiful. Right? But that *hair!* Wow.

Sadly, those pictures are probably the only thing adults have that prove to teens that they were *ever* young, let alone cool. As one of my kids said at 13 when he was frustrated about his parent's rules, "I *know* they were young once… 11, 12, 14. I know they were almost *every* age."

I've been fascinated by the anatomy of "cool" ever since I realized that I *wasn't*. I've come to realize that "cool" is almost always a construct in the eye of the observer, not the actual subject. In fact, despite working with a *lot* of famous people in the film business—Meg Ryan, Kiefer Sutherland, and Patrick Dempsey among them—I have never really met *anyone* who looks in the mirror and sees "cool." Those people whom *others* consider cool are actually often shy, withdrawn, introverted, insecure, or depressed. Their "cool" comes from our inability to read their darker qualities, mistaking their reticence instead as some mysterious or unknown force of calm and detached nonchalance coming from deep reserves of strength or *savoir faire*.

When I got "the film bug" at Oxford University and pulled together a group of talented artists and actors from among the current students, one of them was a young Hugh Grant. Despite being extremely good-looking, he had a uniquely disarming quality of nerdy awkwardness that eventually would take him to superstardom. He is genuinely one of the smartest and wittiest people I've ever known, and he could have played cool. However, he is enormously accessible and likeable by being who he is.

A couple years after we shot *Privileged* with Hugh, I received a call from friend of mine who was casting the latest Bond picture. They were looking for a new, fresh face for Bond and Hugh's name came up. I am not sure ultimately what the reasons were for him not being cast as Ian Fleming's spy, but I'm sure that part of it was that he just didn't project "cool." Good thing for him, because he has had a much more varied film career as a result. As a William Morris Agent famously said upon hearing of Elvis's untimely death, "Great career move."

But let me tell you about the man who may be

considered one of our century's coolest actors— **Robert Redford**.

Upon finishing our not-very-good but "good enough" first feature at Oxford University, my directing partner and friend, Michael Hoffman, wrote a brilliant script called *Promised Land* about an event that happened in his small home town in Idaho. It eventually became a film starring, among others, Meg Ryan and Kiefer Sutherland—but it got a boost from Redford, who had just founded the Sundance Institute.

Redford personally invited us to the second year of the Sundance Institute, and eventually he become my mentor. He was not only the world's top movie star at the time but had just won the Oscar for directing *Ordinary People*—which earned him the ironic nickname "Ordinary Bob" among his friends. He had not only played the Sundance Kid—the ultimate cool character— but *everything* was cool about this guy. He could act, he could direct, he was an environmentalist, an athlete, a philanthropist, a successful businessman. He was one of the most admired people on the planet, and rightfully so.

As we got to know each other, he eventually flew me up to Sundance in a private jet, put me up in his son's room, and asked me if I'd be interested in running his company. I reluctantly had to decline due to prior commitments, but during that "get to know the real me" weekend I also learned that he'd started out as a painter and a baseball player. Was there anything this guy could *not* do?

We remained friends for years and produced two films together, *Promised Land* and *Some Girls*. We were premiering at the Sundance Film Festival in Park City, Utah when I ran into him on Main Street. He was flanked by two burly security guards. I asked him what was up with the security guards. He said that evidently there had been some threats against his life from some crazed, tattooed guy with a Mohawk. *Taxi Driver* had come out a few years before, so I cracked, "Bobby De Niro is after you?"

Not missing a beat, Redford replied dryly, "Yeah, he's jealous of my career." Knowing Redford as I did at that time, I knew the subtext of that comment. De Niro was constantly being nominated for Oscars and was looked as America's greatest actor. Even though "Ordinary Bob" had just won his first Oscar as a director and even though he was a bigger movie star than De Niro, he still did not feel as cool as De Niro.

Imagine that.

A few years prior, I had been lucky enough to land an internship with my United States Senator, Henry "Scoop" Jackson. As a Senate staffer, I would hang out after work with an immensely talented group of staff members from other offices and we would exchange amusing stories about our bosses. On one occasion, one of House Speaker Tip O'Neill's staffers told me of a time when the Speaker was touring the Midwest and ran into this extremely handsome, well-spoken young man in a cowboy hat. The man started thanking the Speaker for his support of the environmental legislation he had been pushing. The Speaker smiled and nodded, knowing that he should know this young man but being unable to place him.

The young man proceeded to tell him about some upcoming legislation and just wanted to ask if the Speaker had any questions. The Speaker shrugged, still unable to place the young man's somewhat familiar face.

Eventually, the young man started to pick up that the Speaker did not know who he was so he politely gave him hints like, "I've bought several acres near Provo and hope to protect the whole canyon. I renamed it 'Sundance' after making *Butch Cassidy and the Sundance Kid*." Again, the Speaker nodded and forced a smile still unable to place the man.

After the young man said his goodbyes, the speaker turned desperately to this staffer and said, "Who was that?" And the staffer who had been cringing the whole time said, "That was Robert Redford." The Speaker nodded, still a bit confused. "Ah."

Upon arriving back in Washington DC, the Speaker

embraced his wife at the airport and said, "Darling, you would not believe who I met. Robert Roquefort." He still didn't have a clue who the man was!

Years later, I told Redford about this story during a taxi ride in London. He laughed his head off, never having heard the backend of this story. Here was a man at the height of his fame who didn't feel the slightest bit cool. He truly was just ordinary. Bob.

When I met Bob's kids and witnessed the "Dad" side of him, the "de-cooling of Bob" was complete. It doesn't matter what you achieve as an adult. That's just not part of your kids' world. In a really back-handed, indirect way, one of the greatest gifts that parents give their children is the opportunity for them to feel cooler than someone else. After all, while kids definitely are on the cusp of trends and know everything about the latest music, they are generally awkward, insecure, acne-challenged, and way too desperate to be cool. "Desperate to be cool." The very words are antithetical.

A friend of mine who is a mother of three boys calls the teen years the "Doofus Years"—but with loving affection and not to the boys' faces. Heaven knows, there are so many forces at work making our kids feel like doofuses that the last thing they need us to do is remind them of it. Good thing that our own out-of-date appearance is there in the hallway to make them look good by comparison!

On the flipside, while I think it's good to

embarrass your kids once in a while with a kiss or a bad dance, parents should not allow the uncool badge to become their identify. You have too much serious parenting and mentoring to do to allow that, and it can create a wedge between you and your kids. The fact is, you are the same person—neither cool *nor* uncool—that you've always been; so don't allow your own insecurities to give your kids too much power as the arbiters of cool. After all, none of them feel that way, either.

So, in conclusion, if none of us actually consider ourselves cool, then does coolness actually exist? Evidently only in the eyes or mind of the beholder—and then only out of some misplaced insecurity encouraging us to compare ourselves to others. And since all of us are "beholders," only we can put coolness in its proper place.

The Takeaway

What You've Forgotten About Being a Kid:
It has never occurred to you that, at one point in their lives, your *parents* might actually have been cool.

What You Can Do About That as an Adult:
Really squeeze every moment out of the time you have with your kids before they realize that you're not that cool. And once their own cool

obsession kicks in, keep it in perspective so it does not become a self-defeating prophecy.

The Birds-Eye View

21 Things You Forgot About Being a Kid

Your future makes you nervous.

HE WAS 15 AND he had a mystery to solve. He had been in the project the last eight years and, a few years into it, began to be plagued by an intense fear of going around corners. He would break out in sweats and sometimes tears—even walking from his room to the bathroom. It only happened when he was alone. This obviously caused a lot of problems for him, so he needed to figure out why.

On the surface, it looked liked a latent childhood "monster under the bed" issue. We are afraid of things in the shadows or in the darkness, or just things we cannot see. However, that normally happens when we are 5 and disappears when we are 10, not the other way around.

Each year he would come in feeling a bit tentative. We would always have a good talk and he would leave relieved, but not until after a good cry. This particular year I was anxious to help him get to the bottom of things. I asked him at what point this started to happen.

After some sorting of details, we identified "age 10" as the point when the fear started growing in him. I asked him what he thought was going to happen. He said, "I don't know," and he did not appear to be holding back anything. He just had a sense of impending doom.

The more I thought about it, the more his answer, "I don't know," seemed to be the key. He didn't know what was around the corner—and that was the issue. I knew that he came from a well-to-do family who lived in a compound. I knew that his life was safe and predictable. I also knew that when he was younger his older cousin had died unexpectedly. Every time I would ask about her, his eyes would well up and it was difficult for him to speak. This time, I pushed him and asked if he had been close to her. He nodded in a way that suggested he had been very close to her. I then said, "I know you don't like to talk about this, but I just need three more pieces of information. How old were you, and how old was she, when this happened? And how did she die?" He whispered, "I was 10. She was 21 and she died in a car accident. One moment she was here, the next she was gone."

With that he sobbed the hardest I had seen him sob.

Suddenly, things started to make sense. Something totally random, dangerous, and unexpected had invaded his previously safe world—and now that he knew such a thing was possible, he was fearful of it happening again.

The fear just manifested itself in corners. He had a form of second-hand Post Traumatic Stress.

He took that explanation in. We discussed how the unexpected could always invade our lives at any time but that the likelihood of such life-altering events was miniscule. We discussed how we can be ruled by fear which is defined as "imagining something that has not happened" or we can keep the risk in perspective and choose to live our lives. We also discussed how he had survived the last crisis and, in the unlikely event one would rise again, he would survive that as well.

When he came in this year he was a different young man—happier, bolder, more confident, and less stressed. He told me that he had not suffered another episode for a long time. By identifying his fear, he had largely conquered it.

Here is another example. The campfires at the Prodigy Camp are the highlight of the experience because they give the teens a chance to come talk about the most difficult thing they've ever faced. One night, a 14-year-old camper was talking about a series of difficult things that had happened over the past two years and how that had created an almost paralyzing fear of the future and the unknown. Since the campers had just learned story structure, I put on my cinematologist hat and asked the tribe: If he is our main character, what is his arc? If his life were a movie—which in the case of any 5000 Days Project kid, it actually is—what does our

main character need to achieve in the end? Several kids raised their hands suggesting that he needed to make his life more predictable or make extra safe decisions to ameliorate the fear. Then, **Diego**, the youngest kid at camp who was also a brilliant rap lyricist, said, "Doesn't he just need to discover the beauty of the unknown and the possibilities of the unexpected?" Wow.

Applying traditional story structure and perspective, the boy was able to see his arc and help create a course for where he needs to go. In *Titanic*, Rose needed to reject the safety of her social position to discover her true self and purpose. In *Star Wars* Luke needed to tame his ego and trust a force much greater than his self. In *The Wizard of Oz*, Dorothy needed to learn that everything she ever longed for had been in front of her all along. All stories are about a journey, and the obstacles the main characters need to overcome—to learn what they need to learn.

Life for a kid is like driving on a mountain road. From the road, they see the beauty of the mountain, the danger of the cliff and the curve up ahead. They have not yet put in the time to automatically gain perspective, so they view things from road-level. That means that what they think lies around that curve is consciously or unconsciously determined by what has laid around the previous curves. That can be good *or* bad; but since they have far more time ahead of them than behind, each and every curve ahead is of vital concern.

This even applies to the kids who appear to have it all—popularity, grades, athletic achievements. For them, corners represent the possibility of losing what they enjoy. For those who worship at the altar of achievement, the fear of failure or not living up to expectations is omnipresent.

Learning to tell our own story, however, automatically gives us a bird's-eye view—or a 10,000-foot view—of our winding mountain road. From it we can see where we've come from and how we got to this point. We see that the previous curves did not kill us. After all, we are still here. We see the curves up ahead. Some are sharp and still in the shadows but most are gentle and easily negotiable. We see our life in perspective.

Personal storytelling helps us make sense of our past influences and future possibilities. It gives us perspective on our lives and enables us to identify our own arcs, defining where we need to go. After all, how are we going to get to where we want to go unless we know where that is?

The Takeaway

What You've Forgotten About Being a Kid:
Your future makes you nervous.

What You Can Do About That as an Adult:
Celebrate or commiserate the full emotion of the moment, then apply your own hard-earned perspective to it—a perspective born out of experience. By modeling the process and sharing your own struggles, you are drawing a roadmap for your kids. They cannot suddenly gain the benefit of your experience, but they *can* learn from the way *you* process what lies around your "corners."

Lesson 21

Wise Guys

21 Things You Forgot About Being a Kid

Eventually, you figure out that you are wiser (and more resilient) than you think you are.

REMEMBER **SIMON**, THE ATHLETIC, smart, handsome and popular kid who self-destructed when his family fell apart? He had sought pain relief in drugs and eventually developed a heroin habit—something from which few individuals ever recover. *Knowing that pain was his master, he decided to set forth on a journey across the United States with only a bike.* Through many aches and blisters ("I discovered that Texas is really big"), he proved to himself who was the master of his pain and proceeded to help the cleanup in Haiti and assist poor Central American farmers in developing sustainable methods of farming. He now owns a sustainable farm in Central California with his new wife.

Remember **Danielle**, the young girl who talked about the joy of puddle-jumping? The one who by the

age of 14 fell into a deep depression and eventually ended up in a mental hospital? *Confronting her memory of molestation, she decided she was not going to allow it so destroy her.* Danielle realized that while you cannot always control that what happens to you, you can control your reaction to it. She refused to be defined by it and has become a strong advocate for women.

Remember **Nicki**, the tomboy who became obsessed with her physical imperfections? The one who

almost starved herself to death? *Realizing that the intense need to control something in her life had become her master, she turned that around, forcing herself to eat one meal at a time.* She is now in University and recently gave a TED talk designed to help other kids avoid becoming a slave to their own fears.

Remember Sophea, the Cambodian boy whose mother died in childbirth and whose heart-broken father abandoned him? Remember how *he decided to confront the pain and seek out a relationship with his father on his own terms*?

Remember **Srey Pel**, the Cambodian girl struggling with the pull between family and being who she truly is? The one who took too many pills this past year and doesn't know whether her deceased mother is telling her to be who she is or to come join her? I usually just ask leading questions and rarely give advice, but I told her that I had envisioned an alternative story. It is a story about a strong, fierce 8-year-old that I met when I first came to Sunrise. She was the epitome of Girl Power and had great confidence. She also fell in love with a girl—who then broke her heart. But then that confidence was shaken when the girl betrayed her and her brothers and sisters rejected her. She wanted family so badly that she listened to them, giving up her true nature and giving up competing in the sport she loved. But then her mother who had never stopped loving her, even in death, let her know that she was proud of her and that it was time for her to make her own choices. And she did. She decided to own who

she was and love whom she wanted. She went on to become a national kickboxing champion and a doctor who saved many lives—lives that would not have been saved had she made a different decision. Eventually, on a kickboxing tour she met and fell in love with a beautiful girl and eventually, her brothers and sisters slowly but surely came back realizing the courage it took for her to be her true self. That was my vision of her.

Her response? *A Mona Lisa smile and a promise to see me next year.* So far so good.

Remember **Diego**? The mafia drained his family of their savings, the stress killed his father, he fell into a deep depression. His mother got him help and month by month he has pulled himself out of state of hopelessness. He has set an ambitious series of artistic and intellectual goals for which his father would have been extremely proud. *He's almost got a year of sobriety under his belt and is approaching everything he does with a new vigor.*

And then there is Britney, who was the perfect Canadian 12-year-old. Cute, talented, straight-A student, figure skater. But perfectionism was her master: "I would skate round and round in circles wanting to jump but

would not for fear of falling." Fed up with the pressure **Britney** *decided to let loose and risk it all, eventually becoming one of Canada's leading Heavy Metal rock stars.*

Gennette was a passionate, beautiful African-American teenager with ambitions of becoming a journalist. However, in her words she had, "Absolutely no work ethic." Soon, the temptations of boys and partying ruled her teen years, and by college, **Gennette** became the central figure in the largest political scandal

of 2011. *Refusing to be a victim of profession she so admired, she rebooted and now works hard, using her writing skills to advocate for the elderly.*

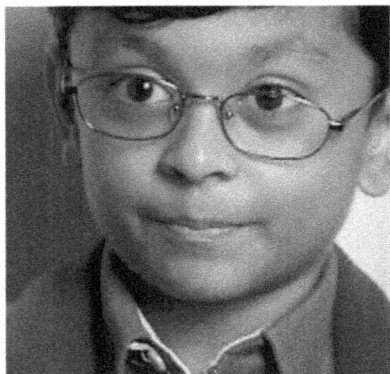

Prottush was a young Muslim boy who immigrated to America just before 9/11. As "his kind" increasingly became the target of prejudice, he retreated from his own identity and lost himself. Soon he had trouble making decisions and actually feeling anything. *Through playing music, he was able to find himself again and now is thriving in the tech industry.*

Henk *loved* video games. They were the foundation of his friendships and a good diversion from having an absent father. As they became his master, however, he

did not like the slothful, dumpy teen he saw in the mirror. *One summer, he decided to drop video games all together, start sailing and get a bicycle.* Before long, his popularity skyrocketed along with his grades. He now goes to a prestigious business school and is plotting to take over the world.

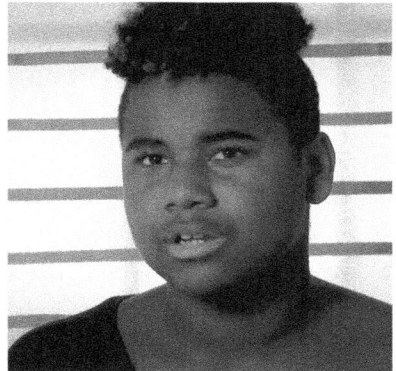

Darius started realizing at 8 years old that he did not feel like other boys. He was drawn to the things girls liked and so, at age 11, he started to identify as a girl. *Against great prejudice and misunderstanding, Darius has refused to be anything other than who she is.* Don't mess with her!

Luciano grew up dirt poor in Chile. His mother abandoned both him and his father. At age 6 he lost his right eye to cancer. When he was 14, he was riding too close to a commuter train, got sucked in under the cars, and lost his right arm and his right leg. In a country where such a condition may doom a person to begging on the street, he realized he had two choices—be angry

at God, or take full responsibility for what happened and never look back. **Luciano** chose the latter and *has become a major para-Olympics star and a national celebrity.* He has refused to let circumstance and bad luck define him. Since losing his right eye, right arm and right leg, he now refers to his left side as his "lucky side."

Interview after interview, I have been blown away by the internal resilience and wisdom of kids. When asked the right questions, they tend to come up with the right answers. This led me to speculate that each one of us must have something akin to an **Emotional Immune System** not unlike our physical immune system.

Whenever we get a cut or a virus attacks our body, our Physical Immune System kicks in, automatically sending in antibodies and other healing forces to bring our body back to its healthy state.

When our amygdala gets stimulated with distressing news or some upsetting event, however, such healing forces don't seem to kick in automatically. We often dwell in darkness, confusion, fear, hatred, resentment, and bitterness until something unlocks that healing system. Over the course of my interviews, I have discovered that that "something" appears to be Emotional Intelligence—something we develop through experience and self-knowledge. Time and time again, I have seen complex problems that can wound or incapacitate someone be solved by simple revelations. Witness Sophea, whose emotional constipation was arresting his development until he processed his sadness. Witness Britney/Kobra who realized only she could release herself from an obsession with being perfect. Witness the Prodigy Camp boy who discovered that he was anger's "you-know-what."

In my case, through cognitive therapy, I came to a realization why I was not meeting the right person. I discovered it was all on me—and the upside was that I had all the tools to fix the problem. I was simply asked the right questions, which led me to discover the right answers.

Can we scientifically point to that as an Emotional Immune System at work within our bodies? No. But as with a black hole, we know *something is there* because of its gravitational pull.

It is essential to point out here that there are serious complex mental health conditions (chemical depression, bi-polar conditions, schizophrenia, narcissism, autism, Post Traumatic Stress, and so on) that can only be addressed with professional help. There are others that are best addressed with the help of a qualified therapist, counselor, life coach, or spiritual leader.

That said, we all have mental health issues—and with depression projected by the World Health Organization to be the number one health crisis facing us as a species in the coming decade, it is time to unleash our own natural healing forces so that the professionals can focus on those who need help most.

Based on my empirical evidence, I would suggest that as many as four out of five of our problems can be solved by developing our emotional intelligence, thereby unleashing this internal wisdom.

So, how do we do this?

A Further Guide to Understanding

LESSONS HAVE BEEN LEARNED. But where do we go from here? What's the *bigger* picture? And we do mean *big*.

We all know about the vast body of scientific data around the benefits of written journaling. Based on my 5500+ interviews on film, I am convinced beyond a shadow of a doubt that the age-old "oral" tradition of telling your story is even more effective.

Witness **Andy**, my nephew. When he was 9 years old, I was staying at his house and he asked if he could become a 5000 Days kid because his older brother and sister were in the project. I said yes, set up the camera in his room, and asked if he was ready. He nodded cautiously…

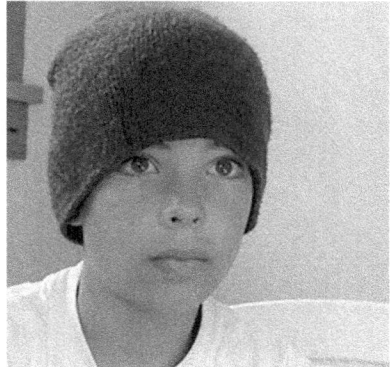

...then immediately burst into tears.

I said, "Andy, are you okay? I haven't even asked you a question yet."

He nodded and said, "I know... but I know what you're going to ask me."

I raised an eyebrow, though this was *not* a surprise. Siblings talk! "Oh, yeah? What's that?"

He replied, "You're going to ask me about the last time I cried, and why."

I nodded. "Well, that's normally question seven—but it sounds like you already know the answer."

He also nodded, and looked at his feet. He took a deep breath, then proceeded to tell me about what had happened three days before in his classroom. He had been cast in the school play and the teacher asked him to stand and sing his solo in front of the class.

As he tried to continue telling me the story, he again broke down crying.

I looked at him, feeling his pain, and told him to take his time. I wanted to hear the story *when* he was ready to tell it. He took a deep breath and tried again only to be overtaken by tears once more. Finally, on the third attempt, Andy was able to get the story out. Basically, what happened was that he stood up, sang his solo, the kids laughed at him, and he ran out of the classroom in tears—the sort of childhood experience that would put you in therapy in your 40s, trying to explain why you are afraid to speak in front of the Rotary Club.

Just for stupid filmmaker reasons, I asked him if he'd tell the story again loud and clear so that I could get it all on film. He did so and had no trouble getting through it.

Suddenly, I got an idea. I asked Andy if he trusted me. He said, "Uhhh, yeah."

I said, "Okay, last time—I promise. I want you to tell me the story once more; but this time, I want you to *sing* it."

He looked at me strangely, then shrugged and started to sing his story. "I was in my class and the teacher asked me to sing my solo..." In a moment he was laughing. Loudly. At himself.

And this is when I saw, firsthand, the value of *oral* journaling. In a very short time, I watched Andy take an event that was so difficult for him that he could not even get it out of his mouth—and I watched him barf up this story, expose it to air, and laugh at it. The same kind of thing happens when we eat

bad food and have to vomit it up in order to feel better. While the process is painful, have you ever felt better relief than when you've thrown up something that's making you feel ill?

Emotions that go unexpressed gain power over us. A brain imaging study by Dr. Matthew Lieberman of UCLA has proved that by verbalizing our feelings of sadness, anger, and pain, these feelings become less intense.

How does this work? As Dr. Lea Waters explains, "As soon as you ask a child to verbalize their emotion, the child accesses their brain's pre-frontal cortex, which is the part they use for language and to process what's happening. It takes them out of their amygdala, the lower part of the brain which is responsible for those strong emotional reactions and helps them calm down because it controls their impulses."

As they taught us in kindergarten, "Use your words." Those teachers were pretty sage.

Stick with me through a discussion of how The 5000 Days Project has formalized this power of verbalization; the technology we have developed to scale the approach; and our full vision for utilization of these tools.

The StoryQ Method

When I was a child, my favorite book was Crockett Johnson's *Harold and the Purple Crayon.*

The plot was simple. Harold, a cartoon boy in a nightgown, lies in bed one night and sees the moon shining through his window. He decides to have an adventure, so he picks up his purple crayon… but suddenly realizes he does not know where to go. So Harold draws a road and follows it. At some point his hand grows unsteady, drawing ripples, and he falls into a vast ocean of his own making. He does not know how to swim, so he quickly draws himself a boat and gets on board. However, the boat will not move, so he draws a sail. Soon he is headed back toward shore where, tired and hungry, he draws himself a tree to create shade, as well as a number of pies to eat. And so on.

Only years later did I realize why *Harold and the Purple Crayon* was my favorite childhood book: *Harold realized that he was the author of his own story* and used his crayon to (literally) illustrate that point.

The world is split in two.

There are the victims—people who lack the knowledge or courage to pick up the crayon; they pass the authorship of their story to others and end up being a secondary character in someone else's story.

Then there are those who pick up the crayon and assume authorship; they have the courage and curiosity to seek answers to the single greatest mystery in their life: "Who in the World am I?"

We designed the StoryQ Method with this goal in mind: To help individuals recognize that *they are holding the crayon*—that every thought, every word, every deed, every action, every day writes their autobiography, in real time.

So how is this best achieved?

The StoryQ Method is all about allowing individuals to discover their own truth through a guided neo-Socratic inquiry—accessing an inherent wisdom within us that can heal the grand majority of our emotional wounds and make us high-functioning and healthy adults. As I have mentioned in connection with our Lessons, we might liken this to a type of "emotional immune system" that, unlike its physiological counterpart, is not triggered by trauma but by emotional intelligence and awareness of trauma and its effects.

While many find their emotions confusing if not frightening, those very emotions actually hold vital clues to what is right and wrong within us. By learning how to read and process them, we can solve many of our own mysteries.

The StoryQ Method is basically about asking the *right questions* in the *right order* and in the *right setting* to help the interviewee discover *their own* right answers.

STEP ONE

This involves the invitation. Prospective

interviewees are asked if they would like to make a longitudinal movie of their own lives by answering key life questions at every stage (normally on an annual basis). Because professional lighting and filming involves expertise, $15k worth of equipment and a valuable hour—our time, and that of the interviewee—I always suggest a "mutual audition." I make clear that we are looking for individuals who are authentic, open, honest, and articulate, and who *want* to be in the project.

On the flipside, we want interviewees to experience the process before making a decision so that they feel comfortable and want to do it. The key is setting the stage for everyone involved to *own* the decision and bring their "A game."

In all of my years of doing this, I can only think of one subject—a 14-year-old-boy—who got into the interview and really did not want to do it. He was clearly suspicious of the process and engaged in a game of witty, cat-and-mouse answers. He was super-bright and was using his humor and intelligence to frustrate the process.

I finally got to the bottom of it. Despite my introduction regarding the decision being in both of our hands, he felt as if his father had "set him up" for something and he was not about to cooperate. As we wound down the interview, I thanked him for giving it a try and told him my experience of the interview. I said, "It made me sad that I was unable to assure you that this was a safe place to share your thoughts and feelings. I, like you, use my wit to steer off authentic questions when answering them would make me feel vulnerable. I have failed you and I am sorry."

He looked at me, taken aback, then looked at his feet. After a moment, he replied, "People have said that before—that I use my intelligence or wit to avoid talking about my feelings. I need to work on that." Given that conclusion, even that interview was not a waste of time.

At the core, the key ingredient is trust. As I mentioned before, the project takes a very unconventional legal approach—we maintain ownership of the actual film footage but leave the story rights with the individual. This means that both parties need each other if the decision is ever made to go public with a story. Hence, there is no chance of using stories for exploitation purposes or revealing things without the ultimate permission of the interviewee. The history of the project has revealed that the grand majority of individuals eventually want to share their stories if they think doing so can help others. They are empowered by sharing something so valuable—even if their stories involve difficult topics like addiction, molestation, eating disorders, sexuality, and the like. But controlling one's story is the guiding principal. This is why we call it a *mutual* audition. Everything is based on mutual respect, and no story gets released without the cooperation of all parties.

That guarantee is bolstered by the second step.

STEP TWO

Next, we establish privacy and confidentiality. For the stories to be truly authentic and honest, privacy has to be guaranteed. I state the following up front: "Your privacy is completely guaranteed. Your story is yours and yours alone. The only exception is if you share something that leads me to believe that either your life or someone else's life is in danger. Then we share what was said with the right people in order to save lives."

I think it is safe to say that the stories from this project are perhaps some of the most intimate and authentic interviews with children ever captured on film. This can be credited to the courage of the participants and the guarantee that the ownership of their story remains in their hands.

STEP THREE

We ensure a private setting, always conducting these interviews in a comfortable, neutral setting well away from the familiar comfort (and pressure) of peers, family, devices, or other distractions.

STEP FOUR

This involves the actual questions presented in the most effective order.

◆ WARM UP

The first questions cover the basics—name, age, where they are from. These allow interviewees to ease into the experience. From here, we may mix up the remainder of the interview depending upon what the interviewee needs to talk about; but what follows is a typical roll-out.

◆ PASSIONS AND GOALS

Almost immediately, we get down to business. For kids this is, "What do you want to do when you grow up?" or for adults, "Are you currently doing what you ultimately want to do?" Some know, some don't; both replies are revealing, and both get them thinking about dreams, ambitions, and expectations. If interviewees intuitively or overtly know what they want to do, saying so aloud is re-affirming. If they don't have a clue, I encourage them to remove all obstacles and let themselves dream the ultimate dream job. A professional billionaire, a movie star, power forward for Barcelona, President of the World… If they can't answer either question, if they can't identify any passion in themselves, then that exposes something deeper that needs to be explored.

◆ PERSPECTIVE

The next series of questions is all about perspective. What has been the best and worst things about the past year? What lessons have they learned about themselves and the world? It encourages interviewees to get off their road-level view—even out of their foxholes *in* the road—and see their current journeys from 10,000 feet.

♦ FAMILY INFLUENCE AND IDENTITY

The next questions are about family. As a lead-in, I typically ask them to describe each member of their families in one word. Because we find our initial identity in our family, each answer is revealing about that identity.

For instance, mom-answers typically range from caring, loving, or nurturing to demanding, bossy, or strict. Sometimes it is distant and descriptive like "drunk" or something reflecting disappointment like "selfish" or "clueless."

Typical dad-answers range from strong, inspiring, or courageous to undependable, selfish, immature, distant, and absent. Sometimes it is just "no comment" which, in itself, speaks volumes. I will then ask about what the individuals enjoy doing with their parents and if they have stories that back up their descriptions.

For siblings, the most popular reply is "annoying," which makes a positive descriptor like "best friend" or "talented" or "supportive" especially revealing.

♦ SELF-IDENTITY

Then comes a big one. Describe *yourself* in one word. This is obviously difficult for most individuals but also helps them reflect and focus on who they think they really are. Some will say "competitive" or "empathetic" or "ambitious," but even a more casual answer like "awesome!" or "confused" is revealing and opens discussion.

The answer is often then the first in what becomes a *series* of words as I follow up with a request to list their own character strengths. This often requires clarifying that the question is about "who you are" not "what you do." Some kids have problems with the apparent egocentricity and possible conceit of answering the question, but when they are asked in a matter-of-fact way, most are able to respond. The answers may include enthusiastic, loyal, committed, ambitious, focused, caring, loving, empathetic, good listener, thoughtful, intelligent, funny, generous, and so on. I find it helpful to then ask for a story behind some of the more important descriptors. For instance, "Can you tell me about a time recently when you were 'generous'?"

Then, on the flipside, I ask, "And what do you need to work on? What can you do better?" Some individuals have never asked themselves this question before and that in itself is revealing. In such cases, I ask, "So, like Mary Poppins, you are practically perfect in every way?" Then they insist, "No… hold on. Let me think."

For a younger child, you can help them identify something by getting them to recall the comment that is often made by parents directly after that parent yells their name: "Tom, be kinder to your brother," or "Juliette, pick up after yourself!" Most individuals know already, however. The answers will range from "controlling my temper, being kinder, staying focused" to "organization, self-confidence, and being disciplined." In some cases the same descriptor is used in both strengths and weaknesses—like "being sensitive" or "particular."

The answers to questions about their strengths are a great launching pad to identify the core of their self-worth and identifying the tools they possess to help themselves and others.

The answers to questions about the things they need to work on provide a great launching pad to discuss their struggles or burdens. They represent an excellent opportunity for goal setting. Articulating that which is your "master" is key to eventually becoming *its* master.

◆ EMOTIONS

The next sequence of questions involves identifying emotions and what elicits them: "What makes you happy? What makes you sad? What makes you anxious or stressed? What makes you jealous? What makes you angry?" Again, encouraging storytelling immediately deepens the understanding behind such emotions. For instance, "I am happiest when I'm playing music. When I'm feeling stressed, if I just pick up my guitar I feel better immediately."

Almost every answer is revealing. If someone says

"Video games make me happy," the comment can reveal anything from simply enjoying a simple escape or diversion to the avoidance of reality and pain altogether. If someone says, "I am happiest when I am helping others," that says a lot about their values and what fulfills them. However, if someone says "I'm happiest when other people are happy," that reveals unhealthy or blurred boundaries under the guise of caring about others.

◆ THE MAIN EVENT

The next area is the most sensitive and requires the most care. I ask, "What is the most difficult thing you have ever experienced?" Younger kids don't like to hold on to negative emotions, so even a simple follow-up question like, "Has anyone ever said anything mean to you, or something that made you feel bad?" may not yield an answer. However, by age 7 to 9, the question starts becoming a powerful reveal because all of us carry some form of childhood trauma, whether it be simple embarrassment or a more severe occurrence like abuse or tragedy. This is often the thing they most need to discuss or put in perspective. Obviously, more traumatic instances as they are revealed provide an excellent opportunity to connect the individual with professional help before the situation results in something potentially harmful.

◆ FEARS

The next questions revolve around fears. As I noted earlier, most kids say, "Spiders." When I clarify that I'm asking less about visceral fears and more about grander emotional fears, they become more thoughtful. Of course, describing fears of abandonment, neglect, intimacy, failure, or embarrassment is beyond the understanding of most 5-year-olds. However, asking them about any "bad dreams" will often tell the story, whether it be monsters in their closet or losing a parent.

For most individuals 8 years old and up, the ability to identify their fears is a direct reflection of their level of emotional intelligence. For instance, the child who has lost a parent for whatever reason is often keenly focused on the remaining parent. When we adopted my youngest daughter Leah, who had experienced neglect thanks to her single-mother's battle with alcohol, Leah had to know where my wife Julie was in the house at all times. Years of hard work went into helping her rewire that part of her brain.

Recently I interviewed a 24-year-old with whom I had started at age 5. He had been a quirky, soccer-playing, happy-go-lucky kid up until age 14, when his mother packed up and left. Thankfully, his father stepped up and did double-duty, as did a number of neighbors and friends. However, during his Freshman year at college, his very best friend ended up hanging himself on the goal post of his middle-school soccer field. Once again, someone key in his life "left him." This set him back and affected his ability to trust relationships until he fully identified and exorcised his fear.

I strongly believe that helping individuals identify their chief fears is the first step in conquering them. As described earlier, all of our stories in movies and literature are about overcoming our greatest fears. Real life is no different. When kids can identify fears, they can gain perspective on their arc—where they need to go. Again, if you don't know where you need to go, how are you going to get there?

◆ LONGINGS

Next, I give them three wishes, which gets to the core of their longings. I tell them that they can wish for anything at all except for more wishes. Some cleverly ask for a genie or box that grants requests. I shut that down. They need to prioritize three things.

Wishes in the past have run from the social…

- ◆ World Peace
- ◆ End to global warming
- ◆ No one goes hungry or without shelter
- ◆ My friend's parents get back together
- ◆ Our team wins the championship
- ◆ That no one would ever be sad

…to the personal:

- No one in my family ever gets sick or dies
- Unlimited money
- That fairies were real
- That I could fly
- I had a dog
- I get to go to Heaven (but hopefully not yet)

The younger the kid, the more specific the wish. Alternatively, I may have a 4th-grade girl in America who wants to be President, while a 17-year-old orphan in Cambodia might wish simply for a bicycle, job, and place to live.

Some kids might have difficulties coming up with even one wish. This often are the same kids who could not identify their ideal future job or even a passion. This betrays either a fear of dreaming or a fear of making a bad decision.

All is revealing.

◆ IDEAL FUTURES

I often follow this up with a question about their ideal future. If they could simply write their future, at age 35 what would they be doing? Where would they be living? Would they be in a relationship and/or have children? I stress again before they answer that they are only limited by their imagination. What follows is usually an important reveal about how much they dare to dream.

♦ ROMANCE

I then ask if they are in love, have a crush, or are in a relationship. No question makes them feel quite as vulnerable as this one, and I can read a lie in their eyes as easily as the large letters on an eye chart. Some individuals absolutely hate the question while others grow to be comfortable with it over time and address it with enthusiasm. I often follow up with a question about whether in the future they plan to get married and possibly have kids. If the answer to *kids* is *yes* I ask, "How many?" Ninety percent of the time, the number of kids they choose is exactly the same number of kids that are in their own family.

♦ HAPPINESS

I then gauge their level of happiness by getting them to rate themselves on a scale of 1-10 with 10 being the happiest. I then ask if they could snap their fingers and change one thing to make that number go up, what it would be. That often reveals the main thing they need to focus on in the coming year, and opens up a chance to verbalize a goal. Recently, one kid said, "I would be much happier if I had a better relationship with my stepmother." Accordingly we explored the potential obstacles, including *her* perceived fears, and plotted a course that would open up dialogue and actions to ameliorate them. He walked away with a measurable goal that might improve his life—and hers.

◆ FAITH

I will often ask a neutral spiritual question like, "If you woke up tomorrow morning and the Creator of the Universe was sitting on your bed, offering you the opportunity to ask one question, any question, what would you ask?" Answers range from "How did it all begin—the origins of the Universe?" to "What is tomorrow's winning lottery number?"

I may even throw in a question helping them identify what they treasure. For instance, "If your house caught on fire and you could only grab one thing, what would it be?" The best answer to this question was given by a 7-year-old who said, "A fire extinguisher?"

◆ IN CLOSING

There are, of course, many more possible questions in the StoryQ Method, but the above are the basic ones; and I always end with a question about gratitude in hopes of sending them off in a positive state of mind. "What are you most grateful for?"

◆ FOLLOW-UP

Finally, I ask them how it was for them—while the experience is fresh in their heads. As I've mentioned, there are cases where kids go away in tears; but even in the face of such "trauma," the overwhelming majority of the responses I receive are positive. As one girl said, "Like a spa for the brain."

The StoryQ Technology

THE STORYQ METHOD AND the personal interviews I describe above have matured in the context of what we call "The Ambassadors Program"—brave kids who are willing to meet with me one-on-one to do the hard work of improving their emotional intelligence… with an eye toward sharing their stories with other kids. In this way, they become ambassadors for the Method, helping other kids see that they are not alone as they "run the gauntlet," and inspiring them toward their own hard work.

But we have also developed technology to apply the method with far more kids than we could possibly meet with one-on-one.

When requests from schools to adopt The 5000 Days Project grew beyond my ability to fulfill them, my father, who was a nationally-renowned educator, came up with the idea of scaling the benefits of the project. Over the next few years, my team developed and tested **The StoryQ**, which is a compact tablet-based kiosk that goes into a private room of a school or organization. Kids are asked key life questions in the precise method described above, with pre-recorded clips of a trusted face posing the questions. Their responses are filmed by the StoryQ and then sent to the safety of a private cloud account until they retrieve it at age 18.

At first, I didn't know if kids would open up to a machine—but almost 300,000 clips over six continents later, we are certain that both kids and adults enjoy and grow significantly from the experience.

While this scalable, automated system can't fully replicate a *personal* interview in which the interviewer can run with tangents suggested by a child's answers, in many cases the experience results in a *different* type of candor and benefit. The biggest barrier to all of us talking to someone is the fear of judgment. With the StoryQ technology, there is no fear, there is no judgment. It's just you and the StoryQ.

The timing is also perfect for this type of delivery and capture. Kids are increasingly comfortable communicating via technology, and we regularly see them talking to the StoryQ as if it were a human. While privacy is a tremendous ongoing concern in media coverage, the reality is that we're all choosing to interact with technology in more and more personal ways.

And the guarantee of privacy with the StoryQ is the same as in the one-on-one interviews: The kids own their stories, literally; but if our keyword-detection algorithms pick up a threat to the individual or someone else, then it is flagged and the material is anonymously reviewed. If it is then deemed to require further action, the individual is identified and contacted to provide help.

Given that 80% of communication is non-verbal, we continue to improve our algorithms to get at that "missing" information, with the goal of making the StoryQ interpretive, marrying it with emerging technologies like emotional recognition software, retinal reading devices, and a series of other tools which can help diagnose and serve mental health issues with game-changing accuracy.

The StoryQ also offers the "I need to talk with someone" button, which is most valuable. Kids have control, right at their fingertip, with the ability to accept help exactly when challenging feelings and thoughts arise. The approach even takes the effort and fear of confrontation out of asking for help. The alert goes directly to a counselor or person in authority who can respond quickly.

A note about the setting of the StoryQ. As we developed the device, we knew that this automated version needed to reflect the same intimate and safe setting of the one-on-one interviews. We were being told at the time, by everyone, that "the future is mobile." Might we develop this so that individuals can do it on their phones?

No.

Phones may be convenient but they do not create

the necessary sanctity of environment that leads to the best experience. They lack quality lighting and sound. They are subject to interruptions and prying ears. The material can easily be lost or compromised. Phones are also the all-too-familiar setting of very disingenuous Social Media platforms, which are the exact opposite of StoryQ transparency.

While a mobile app might be a helpful supplemental tool to populate an individual's story with daily or weekly updates, it simply cannot provide the setting for the best interview experience. A private room or booth in a school, office, or organization yields the best results, without exception.

A Global Mission

BY LEARNING TO TELL the most difficult story we'll ever tell—our own—we develop the tools to tell any story… and learning to tell stories is one of the most essential skills we can develop. Why? Because all of business, education, law, science, math is storytelling. In math, the number 392 means nothing unless a story is attached to it. *Sales* is storytelling.

All of human communication is storytelling. It's the currency of human connectedness. It is primeval, a tradition from the earliest of times around campfires. It's been the key to our very survival.

Learning to tell our own story is essential because every personal story matters. It's our one fundamental contribution to humanity. From the moment we are born we start taking. We take oxygen, we take nourishment, we take space. The one eternal thing of value we can leave is our own story. And given that our own story is a cautionary tale full of mountains and valleys, it follows that learning to tell our own story is the key to a better world. If we each take care of making the content of our own stories the best it can be—and genuinely so—we can change our world from the bottom up. In this way each of our stories is *epic* and *essential.*

On December 26th, 2004 one of the largest tsunamis in history wiped out entire communities across the Indian Ocean, taking at least a couple of hundred thousand lives. Yet on that morning, one of the elders of an aboriginal tribe on a remote island noticed the strange movement of the tides, the stillness in the air, the way the monkeys and birds were behaving; and he recalled oral stories that had been passed down for generations about these ominous signs. He got his people to high ground, and not one life was lost.

Stories save our lives in countless ways. That's why storytelling is primeval. It's in our very DNA.

Yet, currently, over 99% of our stories die with us, never ending up in the archive of humankind. As the proverb goes, "When an old person dies, a library burns down." Think of the pure waste of human potential, knowledge, experience, and wisdom that could improve or save lives! Wisdom that could help us avoid repeating past mistakes. Knowledge and experience that could give us a true picture of humanity—not just a tiny part of it.

Incredibly, the United Nations estimates that as many as 30% of the babies born are *never even registered as being born*. If you live and die and there's no record of you having existed—well, if a tree falls in the forest and nobody is there to witness... does it make a sound?

Add to this troubling fact the observation that history is written by the victors and the privileged few—artists, authors, celebrities... and a smattering of journals and diaries. Beyond registering our birth, marriages, and deaths, only a tiny fraction of us get to permanently record evidence of who we really are.

Social Media once held great promise to democratize this process; but thus far that promise has been largely squandered by companies abusing and exploiting privacy, and individuals using the platform to project the life they *want others to think they are living* versus authenticity and truth. The result? We are not only leaving a dubious legacy but also a lot of *very bad data*.

But what if there were an antidote to Social Media, to the fiction and bad data it produces?

What if there was a type of "Private Media," where every human being could record their authentic stories without fear of judgment? Where the automated interview process itself could give individuals perspective on their lives, grow their social and emotional intelligence, and help them discover their own vital place in the human story? Where individuals could be guaranteed complete privacy and Humankind could tell the truth? And, where *all* of that data is mined anonymously by the growing capabilities of Artificial Intelligence while continuously gleaning wisdom for the good of humankind?

And what it this became the mission we *all* had in common, the duty we all feel honored to perform for the collective good of our species?

The beauty of stories is that they are ultimately the key to both personal and world peace. Divisiveness, tribalism, and fear all fall away once we realize that we have far more in common than we thought. That we are all part of the human family and are fellow travelers on this spaceship called Earth.

J.R.R. Tolkien, in one of his lesser-known works, metaphorically envisioned all of humanity as a choir that only reached its potential when *every* voice could be heard. Imagine...

In 1977, space probe Voyager began its journey out of the Solar System. In addition to its scientific mission, Voyager was also an ambassador of the Human Race, carrying with it a "golden LP" of data representing the best that Earth had to offer: photos, greetings from the

United Nations and President Carter, the cries of whales and babies, works by Mozart and Chuck Berry, indigenous world music, and spoken words in 55 languages. If alien life finds that golden disc millennia from now and comes to Earth to investigate, what will they find if we are no longer here? What legacy will we leave? The slime trail left by Social Media and political pundits? What will there be to say, "This is who we *really* were."?

Can there be a more golden record of our race? We say, *yes*. Yes, there can be. There can be the Human Record, a central repository of every living person's story captured privately and securely on digital video and salted away for posterity.

How would such an ambitious goal be pursued? There are many questions to be answered, but some ideas might include:

♦ Establishing an international volunteer board of the finest minds to create strategies for a vast, AI-catalogued, nonprofit archive, owned by all. These individuals would include leading innovators in technology, economics, politics, faith, and so on. A multi-cultural set of questions would be developed and a plan would be designed to reach the far corners of the world. These questions would be based in brain science dedicated to growing the EQ of all human participants.

◆ Establishing an Ambassador for Story at the United Nations and other international and governmental bodies.

◆ Building a Peace Corps for Story—an army of young people employed to bring story-collecting devices to the most distant places. Or expand the reach and mission of the current Peace Corps.

◆ Bringing together existing organizations which are already collecting stories and add their genius to the cause. For instance, the Humans of New York or the NPR StoryCorps models. The latter has done the most on this front, developing an app, building a few audio storybooths in key cities, and sending around a mobile recording unit. However, with 80% of communication being non-verbal, recording audio only captures $1/5^{th}$ of the truth. In fact, this represents a massive inherent flaw in our current method of surveying, polling, keeping records, and collecting data of the human experience. Over the last two decades, The 5000 Days Project has set the gold standard in encouraging and enabling people to share deep, authentic stories on film. Through its thousands of filmed interviews and 300,000 story clips, the brain-science-based StoryQ method and StoryQ technology have developed the means and expertise to contribute to a global effort in capturing and archiving the human experience.

- Building strategic partnerships using The Library of Congress and its counterparts across the world. Give Social Media platforms the opportunity to contribute and redeem themselves by bringing their expertise and directing their audiences to the cause. Work with an alliance of faiths to tell their stories. Offer the mission and a means to fulfill it to every interested company, organization, and state. Engage every school child in this collective effort to build something permanent for the betterment of humankind.
- Creating a global media campaign designed to build awareness, enthusiasm, and a sense of collective mission.
- Creating Artificial Intelligence to select human stories to be shared with the approval of the contributors. These stories would seek to create tolerance, understanding, and connection, promote world peace, and share the human struggle—letting all world citizens know that they are not alone.

No human left behind undocumented. No life lived in complete obscurity. Every birth a miracle, every story a treasure. Every person an eternal interstellar ambassador. Billions of stories, together creating a Grand Human Choir reaching sonic perfection when every voice can be heard.

Imagine…

Acknowledgements

The real heroes of this journey are the young people who dared to take it with me. In a world where introspection and reflection has been coopted by Social Media, where trust has been eroded, and where shorter and shorter attention spans make big-picture investments a rarity, these young people have had the courage to be different. Thank you all. And to your parents and families. This has been and continues to be the privilege of my life to be a part of yours.

To view the longitudinal films featuring several of the kids mentioned in this book, visit The5000DaysProject.org/films.

To my partners Max, Greg, and Anya, who have brought their immense talents to this vision and upon whom I depend for everything. Greg for editing this book, administrating this global project, and for your unwavering belief in me. Max for sacrificing an unlimited amount of opportunities to help realize this vision with your design talents and for your unlimited pursuit of excellence in all you do. And Anya, for bringing your ingenuity and creativity in sharing this opportunity with the world.

To Dr. John Medina and the numerous professionals and academics whose advice has guided the development of this method and whose wisdom continues to improve it each and every day.

To my mentors: Robert Redford, Stewart Stern, John Medina, Doug Holiday, Ralph Fry, and Bruce Hosford for their investment and belief in me.

To my numerous partners around the world who have given their time and talents to internationalize this movement. Mary-Anne, Elaine, Donna, Geraldine, Alex—you all know who you are.

To Kevin Klar, Andy Maier, Adam MacArthur, Hope Alexander, Rob Burke, John Jeffcoat, Kristi Simkins, Brendan Cescon, and others who have brought their storytelling skills to the project.

To my backers including but not limited to John Stanton, Dan Case, Bill Way, Jolene McCaw, Molly Nordstrom, Susan Lacy, the Seattle Foundation, and the Shoreline Historical Society for being willing to invest in this vision.

To the numerous schools and colleges—especially West Point Grey Academy in Canada, Geelong Grammar School in Australia, and Oriel College, Oxford University in the UK—whose passion to always seek the best for their students has provided a Petrie dish for this project to flourish.

To the teachers who are on the front lines every day, caring for and developing our kids and, who are always looking for ways to improve their game.

To Mom, Dad, and Jody, who started it all.

To Christian Loubek and Dave Rolfe, who inspired this latest chapter.

To my extended family—especially Sam, Luke, Tommy and Joseph—who have put great trust in this process.

To my kids whose wisdom and unconditional love bless me every day; Max and Whitney, who constantly inspire me to be better. Madee, who is always the first to see the dawn in a dark night. Leah, who just keeps beating the odds. And to Oliver, whose courage to be himself gives me faith in all young people.

And finally to the love of my life, Julie, whose wisdom I treasure the most and whose support has provided the fuel for this journey.

Rick Stevenson has filmed over 5500 in-depth interviews with kids and teens from twelve countries as part of a longitudinal project using his StoryQ method of inquiry, dedicated to raising emotional intelligence. He is a creative and passionate combination of award-winning filmmaker and Doctor of Philosophy from Oxford University. He has directed, produced and/or written twelve feature films and 100 hours of television working with Robert Redford, Hugh Grant, Christopher Plummer, Kiefer Sutherland, Meg Ryan, Patrick Dempsey, and others. He's an author, a public speaker, a husband, and a father of four who splits his time between Seattle, Washington and Vancouver, British Columbia.

"My mission," he says, "is to help create a generation of self-empowered game-changers who realize that the choices they make every moment of every day can help them become exactly who they wish to be—to help individuals unlock the power of their own personal story and discover that they can, in fact, be the authors of their own lives."

Bring Rick's message to your organization, and help it transform. Book a speaking engagement now!

rickstevenson.com

www.ingramcontent.com/pod-product-compliance
Lightning Source LLC
Chambersburg PA
CBHW030150310326
41914CB00099B/1786/J